THE PERFECTIONIST'S GUIDE: EMBRACING YOUR INNER DRIVE FOR EXCELLENCE

Pearl C. Hagert

TABLE OF CONTENTS

ACKNOWLEDGEMENT

Big thanks to everyone who in one way or the other contributed to this book. I would like to thank my family for their constant support; To my friends who support my creativity; and thank you to all the mentors and colleagues who shared their wisdom and knowledge along the way. Your guidance, encouragement and faith in me is priceless. Thank you for joining us on this journey.

INTRODUCTION

Have you ever poured your heart and soul into a project and felt like you were "not good enough"? Have you ever set high standards for yourself and then found yourself paralyzed by the fear of falling short? If you said yes, welcome to the club! You may be a perfectionist, but you're not alone.

This book is not about teaching you how to improve your driving skills. It is a part of you and a powerful force. What if we could turn this passion into a great tool for growth and success?

"The Perfectionist Guide" is not designed to lower your standards. It's about learning to control them. We will discover the benefits of your best intentions: attention to detail, unwavering commitment to quality. We will also deal with obstacles - fear of failure, self-doubt, desire to achieve everything.

This book is the way to unlock the true power of success. We'll show you how to:

- Channel your drive for excellence into achievable goals.

- Embrace imperfection as a stepping stone to progress.

- Develop a healthy relationship with criticism and feedback.

- Silence the inner critic and celebrate your accomplishments.

- Find the sweet spot between striving for excellence and enjoying the journey.

Consider the possibilities. Perfectionists armed with this tool will be unstoppable. Let us turn the fire of excellence into a force for good and help you achieve great things. Are you ready? Let's jump right in!

CHAPTER 1

THE ROOT OF PERFECTIONISM

Welcome to the first episode of "The Perfectionist's Guide: Embracing Your Inner Drive for Excellence". In this episode, we'll dive into the roots of perfectionism and explore its profound impact on all aspects of life. From work to relationships and even mental health, we'll uncover the key issues where people strive for perfection. Let's begin the journey together to understand the complexities of being positive and discover strategies for living a better life.

Realizing That Perfectionism Is At The Root Of Many Issues

Perfectionism is often viewed as a desire in society; It is synonymous with ambition and the relentless pursuit of perfection. However, underneath this exterior there is a psychological problem that can cause many problems in all areas of life. In this comprehensive guide, we will embark on a journey that reveals the deep understanding that success lies at the root of many problems. By exploring different ways of doing things, people can understand how this affects their work, relationships, mental health and overall well-being. This understanding forms the basis for positive change and the adoption of a better lifestyle.

Perfectionism is more than a desire to be good; It is a need for complete perfection and a tendency to make mistakes. People who struggle with perfectionism set high standards for themselves and others and constantly strive to meet these expectations. This constant pursuit of success often leads to a cycle of stress, anxiety, and self-doubt as people feel the pressure to succeed in everything in their lives. It is important to know that success is not a good thing to be admired, it is a psychological state that can seriously affect people's health.

In the professional world, excellence can be viewed as a quality that enables people to achieve high standards and produce quality work. But the dark side of perfectionism emerges when people consider the pursuit of perfection. Perfectionists may find themselves spending too much time at work, obsessing over minute details and striving for perfection. Excessive focus on success can lead to endless deadlines, poor co-worker relationships, and ultimately burnout. Additionally, best employees may have difficulty delegating and collaborating, worrying that others may not meet their standards. Therefore, success can hinder the growth of the business and hinder the growth of the business.

Perfectionism can also damage relationships because people hold themselves and others to unrealistic standards. Perfectionists often have high expectations for themselves and those around them, which can lead to constant disappointment and frustration when these expectations are not met. They may have difficulty accepting flaws in themselves and their partners, which can create tension and conflict in the relationship. Additionally, the best employees may have difficulty revealing their flaws for fear that they will be judged or rejected for not meeting their high standards. Therefore, success can interfere with interpersonal relationships and hinder the development of relationships.

The constant pursuit of perfection can be detrimental to mental health. Perfectionists experience stress, anxiety, and depression because they are constantly trying to meet impossible standards. They may engage in negative self-talk and self-criticism, constantly blaming themselves for not being good enough. This cycle of perfectionism can erode self-confidence and lead to feelings of inadequacy and worthlessness. Success can also lead to serious psychological problems such as anxiety, depression, and suicidal thoughts. It is very important that people know the damage done to their mental health and take important steps to solve the problem.

Recognizing that success is at the root of many problems is the first step in breaking the chains. By acknowledging the negative effects of perfectionism on all aspects of life, people can begin to challenge unrealistic patterns and develop self-compassion. It is important to accept failure and celebrate success rather than success. Through self-awareness and self-compassion, people can begin to escape the cycle of perfectionism and live a balanced and fulfilling life. This process may include seeking support from a healthcare professional, practicing mindfulness and self-care, and challenging negative thought patterns. Ultimately, moving away from perfection requires a commitment to self-discovery and personal growth.

The Struggle With Therapists Who Focus On Symptoms Rather Than The Underlying Perfectionist Tendencies

While therapy can be a very effective way to address mental health issues, many people find themselves working with people who focus solely on treating symptoms entirely without reflection. It's the underlying structure that causes these problems. This approach often leaves people frustrated and misunderstood because their therapists fail to understand their success and the impact it has had on their lives. By analyzing this struggle we can understand the problems of finding the right treatment and find ways to solve the following problems.

Therapy is important for individuals who are struggling to cope, providing a safe and supportive environment to explore underlying issues and develop coping strategies. A professional therapist can help people identify the root cause of addiction and improve their thinking and behavior. However, the effectiveness of the treatment depends on the doctor's approach. Some doctors focus only on treating symptoms of anxiety, such as anxiety or depression, without addressing the underlying emotions that cause these problems. Although this approach may provide temporary relief, it does not provide a long-term solution to overcoming success.

For people with a positive outlook, dealing with a doctor who focuses on symptoms rather than the underlying problem can be frustrating. They may feel misunderstood and invalidated, as their therapist fails to grasp the full extent of their perfectionism and its impact on their lives. Instead of addressing the root causes of perfectionism, therapy may become focused on managing symptoms, leaving individuals feeling stuck in a cycle of temporary relief and recurring issues. This can exacerbate feelings of frustration and hopelessness, as individuals struggle to find effective treatment for their perfectionism.

Focusing solely on symptoms without addressing underlying perfectionist tendencies can hinder the effectiveness of treatment. While therapy may provide temporary relief from symptoms such as anxiety or depression, it fails to address the root causes of these issues. As a result, individuals may find themselves seeking to control symptoms without improving overall health. Individuals' efforts to find effective solutions to their problems can lead to feelings of dissatisfaction and dissatisfaction with the treatment.

In order to solve the problem in the best way in treatment, doctors need to know and discover the principles that cause this desire. This may reflect experiences, beliefs, and behaviors that support a positive mindset. By understanding the principles of perfectionism, therapists can help people develop coping strategies and healthy ways of thinking and behaving. Cognitive behavioral therapy (CBT) and acceptance and commitment therapy (ACT) are two approaches that have been shown to be effective in addressing positive outcomes by focusing on beliefs and attitudes.

For those with balance issues, it is important to find a therapist who understands and addresses underlying emotions. It may require finding a therapist who specializes in rehabilitation or has experience working with similar issues. Additionally, individuals should feel empowered to advocate for themselves in treatment and share their concerns and treatment goals. Establishing a therapeutic relationship based on trust and understanding is crucial for optimal recovery.

CHAPTER 2

UNDERSTANDING PERFECTIONISM

Perfectionism is a multidimensional notion that incorporates a variety of actions, ideas, and perspectives. At its heart, perfectionism is the pursuit of flawlessness and the establishment of very high standards, which is frequently accompanied by a critical assessment of one's work and a significant fear of failing or making mistakes.

A perfectionist is someone who has these qualities. They have a tendency to set unreasonably high expectations for themselves, striving for perfection in all of their pursuits, whether academic, professional, creative, or personal. Perfectionists frequently believe that anything less than perfection is unacceptable, which may cause irritation, discontent, and worry when they fail to meet their own standards.

There are several dimensions of perfectionism, including:

1. Self-oriented perfectionism: This is the internal pressure that people put on themselves to reach high standards and avoid making mistakes. Self-oriented perfectionists are extremely critical of their own performance and frequently suffer significant emotions of guilt or humiliation when they believe they have fallen short.

2. Other-oriented perfectionism: This component is holding people to impossibly high standards and being critical of their work. Other-oriented perfectionists may struggle to tolerate others' flaws and may behave in critical or demanding ways.

3. Socially dictated perfectionism: This dimension entails feeling external pressure from others to be flawless. Social perfectionists think they are expected to satisfy impossible high standards imposed by others, such as parents, instructors, or peers. As people attempt to achieve these imagined expectations, they may experience emotions of inadequacy, anxiety, and sadness.

Perfectionism is a personality characteristic defined by a strong desire for faultless results in all aspects of life. Individuals with perfectionistic inclinations sometimes establish unrealistically high expectations for themselves and others, resulting in an endless quest of perfection in their profession, relationships, and personal accomplishments.

Perfectionism may lead to both beneficial and harmful results. On the one hand, it may motivate people to thrive and achieve tremendous success in their pursuits. Perfectionists may exhibit remarkable attention to detail, devotion, and perseverance in achieving their goals. However, the obsessive quest of perfection can have a negative impact on mental health and well-being.

Perfectionists may face increased stress, worry, and sadness as they continually strive for unreachable goals. The fear of failure may be paralyzing, discouraging people from taking chances or attempting new activities for fear of falling short. Perfectionism may also strain relationships by placing unreasonable expectations on oneself and others, resulting in conflict and unhappiness.

Understanding perfectionism entails identifying its numerous aspects, root causes, and possible influence on people's lives. While aiming for greatness is laudable, it is critical to practice self-compassion, accept imperfection, and acknowledge that errors are an unavoidable part of the learning and growing process. Finding a good balance between striving for progress and recognizing one's limitations is essential for overcoming the perfectionist attitude and promoting overall well-being.

Perfectionists are often self-critical and aim for unrealistic levels of perfection, which can lead to emotions of worry, tension, and unhappiness. When they are unable to satisfy their own high goals, they may feel failed or disappointed, which can lead to a cycle of perfectionistic behavior.

Understanding perfectionism entails identifying the underlying attitudes and concerns that motivate perfectionistic behavior. Perfectionists may have a strong fear of failure, rejection, or disapproval, which drives them to strive for perfection in order to prevent these undesirable consequences. They may also have the unreasonable assumption that their self-worth is dependent on their capacity to reach perfection in all aspects of life.

Individuals living with perfectionism should seek help from a therapist or mental health professional to address the underlying reasons of their perfectionistic inclinations and build healthy coping techniques. Cognitive-behavioral therapy (CBT) and other evidence-based therapies can help people question and alter their perfectionism views, reduce anxiety and tension, and learn to accept imperfection and self-compassion.

Finally, comprehending perfectionism requires acknowledging that perfection is an impossible and unreachable goal that can have a negative impact on mental health and well-being. Individuals may create a happier and more balanced way of life by fighting perfectionism and learning to accept and love themselves and others despite flaws.

Identifying Personal Perfectionist Archetypes

Perfectionist archetypes are patterns of behavior, ideas, and attitudes that may shape how you approach activities and goals. As a person, you may show several forms of perfectionist archetypes that influence your thoughts and behaviors.

If you believe you embody the perfectionist archetype:

I. You may always strive for perfection and feel like a failure if something isn't flawless.

II. You may have difficulties finishing projects or do not complete them at all; you procrastinate frequently.

III. You may feel anxious and stressed, unable to relax.

IV. You lack self-worth and self-esteem.

V. You may be dissatisfied with your accomplishments because they are insufficient.

VI. You may think in terms of black and white or all or nothing.

VII. If you do not achieve your goals, you may get depressed.

VIII.   When someone gives you constructive criticism, you may get defensive or hypersensitive.

As an individual, you may discover that you own certain perfectionist archetypes that impact your behavior and views. Recognizing these archetypes helps you better understand yourself and how you approach activities and goals.

One typical perfectionist character is the "all-or-nothing" perfectionist. This sort of perfectionist sees things in black and white: either it's perfect or it's a complete failure. You may feel compelled to accomplish everything correctly or not at all. This can result in severe pressure and dread of failure, as well as an excessively critical attitude toward oneself and others.

Another perfectionist character is the "people-pleasing" perfectionist. This sort of perfectionist is motivated by the need for praise and affirmation from others. You may believe that meeting the expectations of others is necessary to feel worthy or lovable. This might lead to giving up your own wants and ambitions in order to please others, which can leave you feeling angry or disappointed.

There is also the "self-critical" perfectionist archetype, in which you continuously judge and criticize yourself for not reaching your own high expectations. This can lead to feelings of inadequacy, humiliation, and perfectionism paralysis, in which you are so overcome with the fear of failure that you are unable to take any action at all.

Identifying your unique perfectionist archetypes might provide insight into why you behave and think the way you do. Once you're aware of these tendencies, you may start challenging and reframing them to create a better relationship with perfectionism. Remember that nobody is perfect, and you should be kind and sympathetic to yourself while you strive toward your goals and dreams.

So, how can you put a stop to a behavior pattern that other people perceive as favorable but is giving you problems?

The first step is to recognize your own habits. Be aware of your daily activities and when and when you slip into them.

In your personal life, are you reluctant to show others who you are because you are terrified of being rejected, so you believe, "If I'm perfect, no one will reject me?" Do you feel that you are flawed and attempt to cover them up so that others won't reject you?

Recall one or two instances in which you felt rejected. How did you present yourself to others? What was the vulnerability that made you feel that way; your conduct, not satisfying another person's expectations, or something else? Do you feel threatened? Do you believe you are not good or worthy enough for them?

Spend some time with your thoughts and feelings, allowing them to be who they are without judgment. Be patient; it may take some time, but pay attention to how you feel afterward.

Professionally, aiming for perfection might drive you to postpone presenting your product or devote too much time to minutiae, resulting in disarray and hurting your business. Alternatively, you believe you don't have enough time to do it flawlessly, so you procrastinate and postpone starting it altogether. You experience tension and worry as a result of time restrictions.

Do you have a voice in your brain that says, "If it's worth doing, it's worth doing right?" Knowing that this negative self-talk is holding you back from progress, how would it feel to stop? You can; by closing the door properly. You may accomplish this through:

Using self-affirmations such as, "My best is good enough," "Action is better than perfection," and "I'm always learning and improving." My favorite is "Procrastinate Later."

Accept your thoughts, but don't succumb to them.
Record any emotional responses that emerge, and allow yourself to completely embrace them.
When you slow down and search for the underlying cause of your conduct, you will discover that you are compensating for what you lost earlier in life. And it is most likely a belief you developed as a survival mechanism that is no longer useful to you.

When you are in the shadow of the Perfectionist archetype, you may experience difficulties. Stepping into the light is an intentional decision to notice and acknowledge the conduct. Changing your ideas through self-affirmation and visualization is required to reprogram your mind. You may then face your worries and openly express your feelings.

Exploring Different Types Of Perfectionists And How They Manifest

Exploring different sorts of perfectionists may be a fascinating excursion into the complexities of human behavior and thought. As someone who is interested in the topic of perfectionism, you may find it useful to understand the numerous ways in which this attribute presents itself in individuals.

First, there's the stereotype of the "traditional" perfectionist. You can identify with this individual if you have exceptionally high expectations for yourself and others, aiming for perfection in all aspects of your life. Anything less than perfection may feel like failure to you, resulting in constant self-criticism and a never-ending desire for progress.

Next, there's the "adaptive" perfectionist. This type has many similarities to the conventional perfectionist, yet it seeks perfection in a healthier, more balanced manner. You may fall into this group if your high standards serve as inspiration for personal growth and development rather than a measure of self-worth. While you continue to strive for perfection, you can accept and learn from missteps along the road, viewing them as chances for growth rather than disasters.

On the other hand, there is also the "maladaptive" perfectionist. If you are continually immobilized by fear of failure or procrastination as a result of the overwhelming pressure to fulfill unreasonable expectations, you may identify with this kind. Maladaptive perfectionists frequently feel worry, tension, and even melancholy as a result of their unwavering pursuit of perfection. Despite their greatest efforts, individuals may never be happy with their successes, always striving for an unachievable ideal.

There are also "socially prescribed" perfectionists. This type may experience enormous pressure from outside sources, such as family, classmates, or society as a whole, to meet unattainable expectations of success and performance. You may notice this in yourself if you are always seeking affirmation and acceptance from others, focusing your self-esteem on satisfying their expectations rather than your own internal standards.

You may be too critical of yourself in order to fulfill the expectations of others, resulting in a never-ending loop of seeking acceptance and validation from people around you. The dread of failure can be overpowering for this sort of perfectionist, who may believe that their value is linked to their accomplishments and triumphs.

Finally, there are "self-oriented" perfectionists. If you primarily hold yourself to unreasonably high standards, frequently at the sacrifice of your own well-being and relationships, you may fit this description. Self-centered perfectionists may work tirelessly to attain their goals, sacrificing rest, pleasure, and social ties in the process.

Furthermore, studying the many sorts of perfectionists might reveal important insights into the intricacies of human behavior and cognition. Whether you identify as a conventional, adaptive, maladaptive, socially mandated, or self-oriented perfectionist, recognizing your own inclinations may help you establish a healthy relationship with perfectionism and pursue personal progress and fulfillment.

Perfectionism may take many forms in your daily life, impacting your ideas, behaviors, and emotions in subtle yet deep ways. You may detect its existence in the following instances.

1. Setting Unrealistic expectations: You may find yourself setting unrealistically high expectations for your performance, looks, or accomplishments in many aspects of your life, such as job, relationships, or hobbies. These expectations might be so high that achieving them is practically impossible, resulting in perpetual tension and disappointment.

2. dread of Failure: Perfectionism frequently results in a strong dread of failure. You may resist taking chances or attempting new things for fear that you may not succeed right away. This fear might prevent you from seeking possibilities for personal growth and development, trapping you in your comfort zone.

3. Procrastination: Ironically, perfectionism may contribute to procrastination. The dread of failing to reach your own high expectations can be so overpowering that you put off starting jobs or projects until the last minute, expecting for the right time or inspiration to strike. However, this practice frequently leads to greater stress and hurried, substandard output.

4. Overwork: Perfectionists are overachievers who push themselves to work harder and longer than required. You may devote an excessive amount of time and energy to projects, excessively attempting to perfect every aspect and refusing to relax until everything is perfect.

This can lead to burnout, which has a detrimental influence on your physical and mental health.

5. Difficult Accepting Criticism: Even helpful comments or criticism can be difficult for perfectionists to take. You may see each suggestion for improvement as a personal attack on your ability or value, resulting in defensiveness or rejection of input entirely.

6. Strained Relationships: Your quest of perfection might have an impact on your relationships with others. You may expect the same degree of perfection from people around you, creating false expectations and disappointment when they eventually fall short. This might lead to stress and conflict in your relationships with family, friends, and colleagues.

7. Negative Self-Talk: Perfectionism is frequently accompanied by a harsh inner critic who continually criticizes you for perceived flaws or errors. You may indulge in negative self-talk, criticizing yourself for not being good enough or failing to fulfill your own expectations. This self-critical perspective can gradually damage your self-esteem and confidence.

8. Obsessive Attention to Detail: Perfectionists frequently have a good eye for detail and might become focused on little defects or blemishes. You may devote an inordinate amount of time and energy to micromanaging jobs or projects, striving for an impossible level of perfection in all aspects. While attention to detail can be beneficial, it can also stifle productivity and creativity if carried too far.

Overall, perfectionism may infect all aspects of your life, profoundly influencing your ideas, behaviors, and relationships. Recognizing its presence and knowing how to handle it may help you develop a healthy mentality and live a more balanced, satisfying life.

Recognizing Perfectionism As A Compulsion To Bridge The Gap Between Reality And The Ideal

The wrong problem?

Recognizing perfectionism as a desire to bridge the gap between reality and an ideal existence is a critical step toward understanding and managing this tendency. Perfectionism may emerge in a variety of areas of your life, including work and relationships, as well as personal aspirations and self-image. It is generally motivated by a desire to excel, meet high standards, and avoid failure or criticism.

As you strive for perfection, you may place excessive expectations on yourself and others, leading to feelings of inadequacy, anxiety, and self-doubt. The relentless quest of perfection may be draining and unsustainable, resulting in a loop of never feeling content with your results.

It is critical to recognize that perfection is an unrealistic goal and that making errors is an unavoidable component of development and learning. Accepting imperfection may help you develop self-compassion, resilience, and a healthy outlook on success and failure.

By changing your attention from perfection to progress, you may establish more attainable objectives, enjoy minor triumphs, and appreciate the path to your ideal life. Remember that perfectionism is not a measure of your value or ability, but rather an attitude that can be changed through self-awareness, self-acceptance, and self-care.

As you negotiate the complexity of perfectionism, be kind to yourself, seek help from loved ones or a therapist, and practice mindfulness and appreciation to develop a more balanced and satisfying life. Accept your shortcomings as unique features that make you human. True pleasure and contentment come from self-acceptance and honesty, rather than aiming for unreachable ideals.

The problem isn't that you're a perfectionist. Some of the happiest, most remarkable, and contented people on earth are perfectionists. Your problem is how you handle your perfectionism. You are either attempting to remove it or responding to it with punishment. Neither response will work.

The "eradication approach" is just not effective. Perfectionists frequently hear terrible advice such as "just lower your expectations a little bit" or "don't sweat the small stuff." Trying to control perfectionism by encouraging individuals to stop being perfectionists is like attempting to manage anger by asking them to calm down. This strategy has never succeeded throughout history, but it is still widely used. So, perhaps it's time for a fresh strategy.

The "eradication approach" will also fail since self-identification as a perfectionist is an enduring identity marker. We don't discuss perfectionism in episodic terms because we don't experience it in that way. For example, someone may say, "I went through a depression after college," but we don't "go through" perfectionism.

Perfectionism is felt in a profound and visceral sense. Thinking of oneself as a perfectionist is similar to thinking of yourself as an activist, artist, or romantic—it's not an identity you can just abandon.

Perfectionists never stop seeing the disparity between reality and the ideal, and they never stop wanting to actively bridge that gap. The noticing and wanting last a lifetime, which explains the physical attachment to perfectionism. People who identify as perfectionists tend to stick with that identification indefinitely. Trying to get rid of perfectionism is like whacking the wind with a broom.

Perfectionism is too strong for the "eradication approach." When you strive to overcome your perfectionism, all you're doing is wasting energy at the expense of taking care of yourself.

Acknowledging The Comparison Between Men And Women's Perceptions Of Perfectionism In Society

Recognizing the difference between men and women's conceptions of perfectionism in society goes into the complex aspects of gender roles, cultural expectations, and personal experiences. As someone who is interested in understanding these subtleties, let us look at how gender influences how perfectionism is viewed and experienced.

In many countries, there is a double standard regarding perfectionism and gender. Men are frequently lauded for possessing characteristics connected with perfectionism, such as ambition, competitiveness, and . Society generally views their quest of perfection as noble and vital for success. However, this recognition may come with its own set of demands, as males may feel obligated to continuously demonstrate their value via performance and control.

Women, on the other hand, are frequently held to a higher degree of perfectionism than males. They may be lauded for striving for greatness, but they are also expected to conform to traditional gender norms and feminine ideals. This can lead to a paradoxical scenario in which women are pushed to be ideal in certain areas, such as looks or caring, while receiving criticism for being viewed as overly ambitious or pushy in others.

Furthermore, cultural demands of perfectionism might collide with other criteria such as ethnicity, class, and sexual orientation, complicating the picture. Women of race, for example, may encounter specific problems and preconceptions that impact their perspectives on perfectionism.

According to study, women are typically assessed more harshly for their perceived flaws than males. This phenomenon, known as the "double bind," exemplifies the harsh scrutiny women experience when they break from conventional standards of beauty. They may be regarded as overly emotional or incapable of exhibiting vulnerability or making errors, but men are frequently given greater freedom to fail without suffering the same penalties.

However, it is critical to understand that these beliefs and experiences with perfectionism are not universal and can vary widely based on individual characteristics such as upbringing, personality, and cultural background. Other males may feel enormous pressure to adhere to conventional masculine ideals, but other women may find empowerment in defying society conventions and accepting their flaws.

Overall, recognizing the difference in men's and women's views of perfectionism in society necessitates a sophisticated knowledge of the interconnected forces that form our experiences and expectations. By identifying and confronting gendered assumptions and expectations, we can build a more inclusive and fair society in which people of all genders may seek success on their own terms.

CHAPTER 3

EMBRACING PERFECTIONISM

Accepting perfectionism is like walking a tightrope hanging high over a busy cityscape. With each step, the pressure builds, and the fear of failure gnaws at your willpower. However, it has a compelling charm, a promise of greatness, of reaching heights that others can only imagine. So you take the first step, heart pumping and mind racing with possibilities.

You methodically prepare each action, focusing on every detail, perspective, and possible conclusion. It is not enough to just do things well; it is also necessary to execute them flawlessly. And as you walk that tightrope, you understand that perfectionism is more than a personality; it is a way of life.

At first, it's exciting. The joy of pushing yourself to your boundaries and exceeding expectations motivates your every move. You devote your heart and soul to whatever you accomplish, leaving no place for mediocrity. And when you accomplish achievement after success, you revel in the pleasure of affirmation, knowing that your quest of perfection was worthwhile.

But perfectionism is a demanding master who never settles for anything less than perfection. And while you attempt to fulfill its unrealistic standards, you find yourself on the verge of exhaustion, the weight of expectation crushing your spirit.

Despite the confusion and tiredness, there is a feeling of purpose, a sense of accomplishment that comes from knowing you gave it your best. You may slip and fall along the road, but each setback simply strengthens your will to rise again, stronger and more resilient than before.

And as you continue to walk that tightrope, you understand that perfectionism isn't about being faultless; it's about accepting your flaws, learning from your failures, and aiming for excellence in all you do. It is about discovering beauty in the journey, not just the goal.

So you take a deep breath, bracing yourself for the trials ahead, knowing that no matter how difficult the route may be, you have what it takes to accept excellence and make it your own. And when you look out at the enormous expanse of possibilities before you, you can't help but experience a rush of exhilaration, awe at the limitless possibility that is within your reach.

Learning To See Perfectionism As A Strength Rather Than A Flaw

Learning to perceive perfectionism as a strength rather than a weakness is like unearthing a hidden gem behind layers of doubt and self-criticism. At first, it may appear elusive, shrouded by fear of failure and the dogged pursuit of impossible goals. However, as you go deeper, you begin to see its actual potential, its ability to propel you to perfection and encourage others to do the same.

You learn that perfectionism is more than simply expecting perfection from yourself; it is about holding yourself to a higher standard and pushing yourself to go above and beyond what you believed was possible. It requires a strong eye for detail, a never-ending desire to develop, and an unyielding devotion to quality.

As you adopt this viewpoint, you begin to perceive perfectionism not as a cause of tension and worry, but as a guiding light that illuminates the route to your objectives and desires. You learn to channel this energy into your job, where it fuels your creativity and inventiveness.

Instead of viewing mistakes as failures, you begin to see them as chances for development and learning. You realize that perfectionism does not imply being faultless, but rather aiming for excellence in all you do, understanding that each failure gets you one step closer to mastery.

And as you build this perspective, you will discover that perfectionism becomes a source of power, driving you ahead in the face of hardship while motivating people around you to do the same. You become a shining example of greatness, teaching others what is possible when they dare to dream large and follow their interests with steadfast dedication.

So you accept perfectionism not as a burden, but as a gift to treasure—a continual reminder of your potential and testament to your unwavering pursuit of excellence. And as you progress, you learn that true perfection rests not in flawlessness, but in the constant pursuit of greatness, fuelled by an unflinching belief in yourself and your capacity to do everything you set your mind to.

As you explore more into the concept of perfectionism as a strength, you'll understand that it's not just about the end result—it's also about the process. You recognize that the quest of excellence is a continuous effort to improve and refine.

With this newfound viewpoint, you begin to see the beauty in imperfection. You recognize that perfectionism does not imply never making errors; rather, it entails learning from them and using them as stepping stones to greater achievement. You believe that failures should be viewed as chances for growth and development rather than obstacles.

Furthermore, you begin to realize how perfectionism may drive invention and creativity. Instead of suffocating your creativity with self-doubt and fear of failure, you channel your perfectionist inclinations into fueling your imagination and pushing the limits of what is possible. You focus your attention to detail on your craft, resulting in work that is not only technically skilled but also full of passion and creativity.

As you progress on this path, you'll notice that perfectionism becomes a source of incentive rather than worry. You no longer regard it as a weight to carry, but rather as a guiding principle that inspires you to strive for greatness in all aspects of life.

Furthermore, you learn to notice how your desire for perfection affects people around you. Your commitment to your trade motivates others to do the same, resulting in a ripple effect of greatness that spreads far beyond yourself. You become a role model for others, demonstrating what is possible when they accept their perfectionist inclinations and utilize them to drive their objectives.

Finally, learning to perceive perfectionism as a strength entails accepting yourself and utilizing your natural desire for excellence in order to reach your greatest potential. It is about striking a balance between aiming for perfection and embracing imperfection, knowing that genuine greatness is found not in being faultless, but in the constant pursuit of excellence.

Transforming Maladaptive Perfectionism Into Adaptive Perfectionism

Transforming maladaptive perfectionism into adaptive Perfectionism requires using a variety of tools and strategies to guide your personal growth. Let's examine these tools in detail:

Update your mind: The first tool for Perfectionism is to update your mind. This includes changing your mindset from success to achievement. Instead of seeing mistakes as failures, look at them as opportunities to learn and grow. Accept the idea that success is impossible but success is possible. By changing your mindset, you will develop patience and have a better relationship with success and failure.

Self-Compassion Practice:

Self-compassion is the practice of treating yourself with kindness and understanding, especially in times of difficulty or failure. It involves accepting your flaws without judgment and showing yourself the care and support you would give a friend. Research shows that self-pity increases depression and increases depression during depression. So be kind to yourself, celebrate your successes, and learn from your mistakes with kindness and understanding.

Setting Goals:

Another important tool for Perfectionism is to set realistic goals. Instead of striving for perfection, focus on setting achievable, meaningful goals that align with your values and priorities. Break larger goals into small, manageable steps and celebrate each milestone along the way. By setting realistic goals, you will reduce the pressure to achieve and increase your motivation and confidence to follow your dreams. Embracing Perfection: Embracing perfection is an important aspect of adaptive perfectionism. It involves letting go of unrealistic expectations of success and accepting yourself as you are, warts and all. Realize that making mistakes is part of the learning process and an opportunity for growth. By accepting negativity, you will develop your patience, authenticity, and self-acceptance, which will lead to greater understanding and success.

Develop self-awareness:
Self-awareness is the ability to recognize and understand one's own thoughts, feelings, and behaviors. It is a powerful tool for changing maladaptive perfectionism because it allows you to identify when idealistic thoughts arise and how they affect your mental and emotional state. Practice mindfulness practices such as meditation or journaling to gain self-awareness and a deeper understanding of yourself. Seeking Support: Transitioning from bad to good is not a process you can do alone. Seek support from friends, family, mentors, or healthcare professionals who can provide support,

guidance, and perspective along the way. Share your struggles and successes with others and find support during difficult times. Remember, asking for help is a sign of strength, not weakness.

Gratitude Practice:
Gratitude is the practice of noticing the good things in life and focusing on what you have rather than what you don't have. It is a powerful tool that can transform your thoughts from great success to satisfaction and happiness. Take time each day to think about the things you are grateful for, whether it's your health, your relationships, or simple pleasures like a beautiful sunset or a nice cup of coffee. By cultivating gratitude, you will develop a positive outlook on life and reduce the pressure to succeed.

Learn from Failure:
Failure is inevitable on the path to successful change, but what matters most is how you respond. Instead of looking at failure as an expression of your value or ability, view it as an

opportunity to grow and learn. Think about mistakes, what you can learn from the experience, and how you can improve in the future. As a teacher, you will develop patience and perseverance in the face of challenges by viewing failure as more than a personal flaw.

Set Boundaries:
Setting boundaries is important to maintain balance and prevent violence. Learn to say no to demands or expectations, whether they come from others or yourself. Prioritize your physical, mental and emotional health and make time for self-care, relaxation and activities that bring you pleasure. By setting boundaries, you will preserve your energy and focus on what is important to you rather than trying to meet unrealistic standards of success. Self-Reflection Practice:

Self-reflection is the process of examining your thoughts, feelings, and behaviors with curiosity and an open mind. It is a valuable tool that can help you understand your success patterns and identify areas for growth and development. Take regular time to reflect on your experiences, challenges, and successes and consider how they align with your values and goals. By practicing self-reflection, you will develop a deeper understanding of yourself and the self-awareness needed to transform negative experiences into positive ones.

In summary, transforming maladaptive perfectionism into adaptive perfection requires a combination of change, self-compassion, purpose, embracing imperfections, self-awareness, and seeking support. Moving on, gratitude, learning from failure, setting boundaries, and self-reflection. By integrating these tools into your daily life, you will increase efficiency, accuracy, and happiness and move towards a better, more balanced lifestyle. Remember, personal development is not about success; it's about embracing your humanity and striving to be your best self.

Finding Ways To Work With Perfectionism Rather Than Against It

Finding ways to work with perfectionism rather than opposing it is the key to transforming maladaptive perfectionism into positive change. Don't try to break it. for the sake of success. Let's examine some ideas for working with perfection:

Motivation to Work: Perfectionists are generally motivated people who strive for perfection in everything they do. Instead of seeing this drive as a burden, see it as a source of motivation to pursue your goals with passion and determination. Setting ambitious but realistic goals that will challenge you to reach your comfort zone and unlock your full potential.

Set High Standards: The best employees are those who pay attention to detail and demonstrate a commitment to excellence. Don't look at this as a negative, look at it as a strength and set high standards for yourself and your business. Do your best to achieve perfection, but accept that perfection cannot be achieved. Aim for progress and improvement, not perfection, and celebrate success along the way.

Embrace iterative improvement: The Perfectionists often fall into the trap of trying to get everything right on the first try. Instead of trying to be perfect from the start, embrace the concept of backward improvement. Assign larger projects or smaller, more manageable projects and focus on making progress over time. View feedback as an opportunity to grow and improve, and be willing to review and improve your work over time.

Cultivate flexibility: Perfectionists tend to think rigidly and resist change. Instead of adhering to rigid standards or expectations, be flexible and open to new ideas and thoughts. Follow the process of experimentation and discovery, and be willing to adjust your approach as needed. Realize that success does not equal tension and learn to embrace the beauty of the negative and negative.

Practice Self-Love: Perfectionists are often their harshest critics and are quick to judge themselves for perceived shortcomings or failures. Instead of blaming yourself for mistakes or setbacks, show yourself compassion, be kind and understanding. Understand that you are human and making mistakes is part of the learning process. Show yourself the same care and support that you would give to a friend facing similar problems.

Seek support and accountability: Perfectionism can be isolating because people may be reluctant to share their struggles or seek help from others. Instead of suffering in silence, get support and accountability from friends, family, or a mentor. Share your goals and desires with trusted people who can provide support, guidance and perspective. Surround yourself with a supportive community that understands and appreciates your strengths and challenges.

Balancing Ambition and Self-Care:
Perfectionists often have difficulty finding a balance between ambitious goals and the need for self-care and relaxation. Instead of basing your happiness on the pursuit of perfection, prioritize self-care and balance in your life. Whether it's exercise, hobbies, or spending time with loved ones, make time for activities that nourish your mind, body, and soul. Know that taking good care of yourself is essential for success and happiness.

Embrace Imperfections: Finally, remember that perfectionism is not about being perfect; It's about finding excellence while accepting challenges. Look at imperfections not as failures but as opportunities for growth and learning. Embrace the beauty of imperfection and the richness of the human experience and allow yourself to take risks, make mistakes and recover from them. By accepting flaws, you will unlock your full potential and thrive in your personal and professional life.

In summary, finding ways to work with perfectionism rather than fighting it means encouraging it, setting high standards, encouraging improvement, simplifying, practicing self-compassion, seeking support and responsibility, balancing emotions with self-care, and accepting discomfort. Perfect,By incorporating these ideas into your life, you will change the way you do things by influencing a powerful network on your path to positive change.

CHAPTER 4

FINDING BALANCE AND JOY

Your attention to detail and relentless pursuit of perfection has brought you success and recognition, but it has also come at a cost. It's time to embrace your inner drive for excellence in a healthy way. It's time to find balance and joy in your pursuit of perfection.

First and foremost, it's important to understand that perfection is an unattainable goal. No matter how hard you try, there will always be room for improvement. Accepting this fact is the first step in finding balance and joy in your life. Instead of fixating on perfection, focus on progress. Celebrate your successes and acknowledge what you still need to work on, without beating yourself up for not being perfect.

As a perfectionist, you tend to have very high

expectations for yourself and those around you. While this can push you to achieve great things, it can also lead to disappointment and frustration. Learn to set realistic expectations for yourself and others. Recognize that mistakes are a part of life and use them as opportunities to learn and grow. Don't let your fear of failure hold you back from trying new things or taking on challenges.

Another important aspect of finding balance and joy as a perfectionist is learning to let go. You can't control every outcome or situation, and trying to do so will only bring you more stress and anxiety. Learn to prioritize and focus on the things that truly matter to you. Be okay with saying no to things that don't align with your values or goals. Allow yourself to delegate tasks and trust others to do them well, even if it's not to your level of perfection.

It's also crucial to take care of yourself. As a perfectionist, you may tend to put your own needs and well-being on the backburner in pursuit of perfection. This can lead to burnout and diminish your joy in life. Make time for self-care and do activities that bring you joy and relaxation. Whether it's reading a book, going for a walk, or spending time with loved ones, prioritize activities that help you recharge and find balance.

Remember, perfection is not the end goal. Happiness and fulfillment should be your ultimate goals. Embrace your imperfections and learn to enjoy the journey towards excellence. Be kind to yourself and recognize that your worth is not tied to how perfect you are or how much you accomplish.

Finding balance and joy as a perfectionist is an ongoing process. It takes time and effort to shift your mindset and let go of unhealthy perfectionistic tendencies. Be patient with yourself, and remember that progress, not perfection, is the goal. Embrace your inner drive for excellence, but don't let it consume you. With a little self-compassion and a healthy perspective, you can find the balance and joy you've been seeking.

Embracing The Energy Of Perfectionism And Using It To Lead An Inspired Life

You wake up every morning with a fire inside of you; a drive to be the best, to achieve the highest level of success, to strive for perfection. Your mind is constantly racing with ways to improve, to excel, to reach your goals. You are a perfectionist, and you wouldn't have it any other way.

Being a perfectionist can often be seen as a negative trait, with the common belief that it leads to stress, anxiety, and burnout. However, what if I told you that embracing your inner perfectionist can actually lead to an inspired, fulfilling life? Yes, you read that right; your perfectionism can be used to ignite your passion, drive your motivation, and lead you to greatness.

So, how can you harness the energy of

perfectionism and use it to lead an inspired life? It all starts with understanding and accepting yourself as a perfectionist.

Embrace Your Natural Tendencies:
As a perfectionist, you have a natural inclination towards setting high standards for yourself. This means that you have a strong desire to do things well and to do them perfectly. Instead of seeing this as a flaw, embrace it as your unique strength. Your high standards can push you to continuously improve and achieve your goals.

Focus on the Process:
Perfectionists often get caught up in the end result and can become overly critical of themselves when they don't reach their desired outcome. However, instead of fixating on the end result, shift your focus to the process. Appreciate the small victories, celebrate your progress, and be proud of your efforts, regardless of the outcome.

Use Your Perfectionist Traits to Your Advantage:

Your perfectionism can lead to a strong attention to detail, organization, and a drive for efficiency. Use these traits to your advantage in your daily life. Set achievable and specific goals, create a plan of action, and break tasks down into smaller, more manageable steps. This will not only help you reach your goals, but it will also ease some of the stress and pressure that often accompanies perfectionism.

Embrace Imperfection:

Perfectionism can often lead to the fear of failure and the need for control. However, it's important to remember that perfection is an impossible standard. Instead, embrace imperfection as a part of the journey. Accept that making mistakes and encountering obstacles is a natural part of the process. Learn from these experiences and use them to fuel your growth and development.

Find Balance:

It's important to strike a balance between

striving for excellence and allowing yourself to relax and enjoy the present moment. Perfectionists can often become consumed by their pursuits and forget to take breaks, leading to burnout. Schedule in time for self-care, hobbies, and spending time with loved ones. This will not only help you maintain a healthy balance, but it will also provide a necessary recharge for your mind and body.

Being a perfectionist does not have to be a burden or a negative aspect of your personality. Embrace your inner drive for excellence and use it to lead a fulfilling and inspired life. Allow yourself to make mistakes, enjoy the process, and find a healthy balance. By doing so, you will not only achieve your goals, but you will also find joy and satisfaction in the journey. So go out there and let your inner perfectionist shine. You've got this!

Understanding That Acknowledging The Desire For More Is An Act Of Boldness

As a perfectionist, you constantly strive to be the best version of yourself. You have high standards and expectations, not just for others, but mostly for yourself. You tirelessly pursue excellence and are constantly searching for ways to improve and perfect your skills. While these qualities can lead to great achievements, they can also bring a lot of pressure and stress.

But have you ever thought about why you have this inner drive for perfection? Why do you always want to do better and achieve more? It's because you have a desire for more in life. And embracing this desire is not a weakness, but an act of boldness.

Many people might see your perfectionist tendencies as a flaw or a sign of insecurity. They might think that you are never satisfied and always chasing an unattainable goal. But the truth is, your desire for more is what pushes you to keep moving forward, to constantly evolve and grow as a person. It is what makes you take risks and step out of your comfort zone.

Acknowledging this desire for more is a bold act because it requires vulnerability. It means accepting that you are not perfect and that there is always room for improvement. It also means facing your fears and insecurities, and being open to criticism and failure. But through this vulnerability, you gain strength and resilience. You learn to embrace your imperfections and use them as a stepping stone towards your goals.

Embracing your inner drive for excellence also means being aware of your priorities. As a perfectionist, you tend to have a long list of tasks and goals to accomplish. But it's important to understand that not everything is equally important. You need to prioritize what truly matters to you and focus your energy and effort on those things. This way, you can achieve excellence in the areas that truly align with your values and goals.

It's also crucial to have a healthy and balanced approach towards your desire for more. Too much of anything can be harmful, and this applies to perfectionism as well. You must learn to give yourself permission to take breaks and rest, without feeling guilty or anxious. Remember that your mental and physical well-being is just as important as your achievements.

As a perfectionist, you tend to be hard on yourself and often set unattainable standards. But it's important to realize that perfection is an illusion. There will always be something more to achieve or improve. And that's okay. Instead of constantly striving for perfection, focus on progress and growth. Learn to celebrate your accomplishments, no matter how small they may seem.

In the end, embracing your inner drive for excellence is about finding a balance between pushing yourself to be better and accepting yourself for who you are. It's about understanding that you are enough, just as you are, but you still have the potential to be even more. It's a continuous journey of self-discovery and self-improvement, and each step you take towards it is an act of boldness.

So dear perfectionists, do not see your desire for more as a burden, but as a strength. Embrace it, use it to your advantage, and you will achieve greatness. Always remember that your worth is not defined by your achievements, but by who you are as a person. Keep striving for excellence, but don't forget to enjoy the journey.

Realizing that the energy you bring into a room is more valuable than perceived accomplishments and failures

From a young age, perfection is seen in everything you do. Whether it was getting straight A's in school or being the star player on the soccer team, you pushed yourself to be the best. And it paid off; you achieved success and recognition, and people looked up to you.

But as you grew up, you began to realize that your drive for perfection came with a hefty price tag. You were constantly stressed, anxious, and never satisfied with your accomplishments. Your inner perfectionist demanded only the best, and anything less was considered a failure. It was an exhausting and never-ending cycle.

It wasn't until one day, as you were entering a room, that your perspective shifted. You were about to give a presentation to a group of colleagues, and as you walked in, you could feel the tension and nervous energy in the room. But instead of letting it consume you, you take a deep breath and remind yourself that the energy you bring into a room is more valuable than any perceived accomplishments or failures.

In that moment, you realized that your self-worth and value as a person shouldn't be solely based on your achievements. It's about the energy and positivity you radiate, the kindness and compassion you show towards others, and the impact you have on the people around you.

Embracing your inner drive for excellence doesn't mean beating yourself up over every little mistake or constantly striving for perfection. It means understanding that your drive for excellence is a valuable trait, but it's only one aspect of who you are as a person. You are so much more than your accomplishments and failures.

By shifting your focus from external validation to internal validation, you can free yourself from the crippling pressure of perfectionism. It's about finding a balance between striving for excellence and being kind to yourself when things don't go as planned.

Realizing the importance of your energy and the impact it has on others also allows you to appreciate the journey rather than just the end result. The process of growth and learning is just as valuable, if not more, than the end goal. It's about enjoying the ride and being present in the moment, rather than constantly striving for the next achievement.

As you continue on your journey as a perfectionist, remember that your inner drive for excellence is a valuable trait, but it's only one aspect of who you are. Embrace your imperfections, be kind to yourself, and focus on the energy you bring into every room you enter. In doing so, you'll not only continue to achieve success, but you'll also find a sense of fulfillment and inner peace.

Recognizing The Value Of Balance And Self-care

Your drive for excellence and attention to detail is truly admirable. However, have you ever stopped to consider that your constant pursuit of perfection may be taking a toll on your well-being? In a society that constantly praises productivity and success, it can be easy to forget the importance of balance and self-care.

First and foremost, it is important to understand that striving for perfection is not necessarily a bad thing. In fact, it can be a great motivator and lead to success in various aspects of your life. However, when perfectionism becomes all-consuming, it can lead to burnout, anxiety, and other mental health issues. This is where the concept of balance comes into play.

Balance means finding the right amount of time and energy to put into your pursuits, while also making time for rest, relaxation, and self-care. As a perfectionist, it may be difficult to let go of your high standards, but it is crucial for your well-being. Remember that perfection is not attainable, and striving for it may only lead to disappointment and self-criticism.

Recognizing the value of balance also means understanding that you are not defined by your achievements. As a perfectionist, you may have a tendency to tie your self-worth to your accomplishments. However, it is important to remember that you are so much more than what you achieve. Take time to appreciate your other qualities, such as your relationships, hobbies, and personal growth. These aspects of your life are equally as important as your professional or academic pursuits.

Moreover, self-care should be a top priority for any perfectionist looking to find balance in their life. It may sound counterintuitive, but taking care of yourself physically, mentally, and emotionally can actually improve your productivity and drive for excellence. This means developing healthy habits such as exercise, proper nutrition, and getting enough rest. It also means setting boundaries and learning to say no when you are feeling overwhelmed.

It is important to remember that finding balance and practicing self-care is a constant journey, rather than a one-time accomplishment. As a perfectionist, you may feel the need to constantly be improving and achieving, but it's important to give yourself permission to take breaks and prioritize your well-being.

Therefore, recognizing the value of balance and self-care is essential for embracing your inner drive for excellence. It allows you to maintain a healthy and fulfilling life, while still pursuing your goals and passions. So go ahead, strive for perfection, but always remember to find balance and make time for self-care. You deserve it, perfectionist.

CHAPTER 5

LEVERAGING PERFECTIONISM

As a perfectionist, you know exactly what it means to strive for excellence in everything you do. From the smallest tasks to the biggest projects, you have an inner drive to constantly improve and create something flawless. However, while perfectionism can be a positive quality, it can also be a double-edged sword. When taken to the extreme, it can lead to feelings of anxiety, self-doubt, and even hold you back from achieving your full potential. That's why it's important to learn how to leverage your perfectionism in a healthy and productive way.

First, let's look deeper into what perfectionism really means. Perfectionism is defined as a personality trait characterized by striving for flawlessness and setting excessively high standards for oneself. While this may seem like a positive trait, it can also lead to a constant fear of failure and a never-ending cycle of self-criticism. As a perfectionist, you may find yourself constantly striving for an unattainable level of perfection, leading to feelings of inadequacy and disappointment when you inevitably fall short.

However, the key to leveraging your perfectionism is to understand that it is not about being perfect at all times. Instead, it's about striving for excellence and growth. It's about setting realistic and achievable goals, and continuously improving yourself. By shifting your mindset from perfection to progress, you can use your inner drive for excellence to your advantage.

One way to embrace your perfectionism is to recognize its positive qualities. Perfectionists are known for their attention to detail, their strong work ethic, and their ability to focus on their goals. These qualities are highly valuable in both personal and professional settings. As a perfectionist, you have the potential to excel in any field you choose, as long as you learn to channel your perfectionism in a healthy and productive way.

To do this, it's important to practice self-compassion. As a perfectionist, you may be your own harshest critic. You may hold yourself to impossibly high standards and beat yourself up when you fall short. But by showing yourself kindness and understanding, you can break this cycle and learn to accept mistakes as a natural part of the learning process. This will not only help you to manage your anxiety and self-doubt but also enable you to bounce back from setbacks and continue moving forward.

Another helpful tip is to prioritize your tasks and goals. Perfectionists often have a long list of things they want to accomplish, but trying to do everything at once can be overwhelming and ultimately counterproductive. Instead, take the time to prioritize your goals and focus on the most important ones first. This will not only help to manage your perfectionism but also allow you to give each task the full attention it deserves.

Finally, don't be afraid to ask for help. Perfectionists tend to be independent and may have difficulty delegating tasks to others, fearing that they will not be done to their standards. However, learning to delegate and collaborate can actually improve the quality of your work and reduce your workload. It also shows humility and a willingness to learn from others, which are important traits for personal and professional growth.

In summary , as a perfectionist, it's important to embrace your inner drive for excellence while also learning to manage and leverage it in a healthy way. By recognizing its positive qualities, practicing self-compassion, and prioritizing your goals, you can use your perfectionism to achieve great things. Remember, it's not about aiming for flawlessness, but about striving for progress and continuous growth. Embrace your perfectionism and use it to attain your full potential.

Celebrating The Unique Attributes That Perfectionists Bring To The Table

You have always been driven by a desire for perfection. From a young age, you were praised for your attention to detail and your determination to succeed. As you grew older, this drive for excellence only intensified, making you a self-proclaimed perfectionist.

But being a perfectionist often comes with a negative connotation – people may see you as too rigid, too critical, or too hard on yourself. However, it's time to shift that perspective. As a fellow perfectionist, I am here to tell you that your unique attributes are something to be celebrated, not shunned.

First and foremost, perfectionists are known for their attention to detail. You have a keen eye for even the smallest of mistakes and take great care in ensuring that everything is just right. This quality can be extremely beneficial in many areas of life, whether it's in your career or personal relationships. Your detailed-oriented nature allows you to produce high-quality work and shows that you care deeply about what you do.

Additionally, perfectionists are also highly organized individuals. You thrive on structure and planning, making you an excellent leader. Your ability to stay organized and on top of things is a valuable skill, often leading to successful outcomes and projects. Your organization also extends to your personal life, making you a reliable and dependable friend and family member.

Moreover, perfectionists have an inherent drive for excellence. Your inner motivation pushes you to constantly strive for improvement, never settling for anything less than perfect. This attribute can be seen as a positive quality, as it shows your determination and dedication to your goals. Your drive for excellence can inspire others to do their best and can lead to great accomplishments.

Being a perfectionist also means that you have high standards for yourself and those around you. This may lead to some conflicts or disappointments, but it also means that you hold yourself and others to a high level of excellence. Your standards are what push you to be the best version of yourself, and they can also elevate those around you.

Perfectionists also tend to be very detail-oriented, which can be seen as a valuable skill. You have a knack for noticing even the smallest of details, leading to thorough and accurate work. This quality is highly sought after in many industries and can open up opportunities for you.

Lastly, perfectionists have a strong work ethic. Your drive and determination to succeed means that you are willing to put in the extra time and effort to achieve your goals. This work ethic not only benefits you, but it also sets a great example for those around you.

Embracing your inner perfectionist means embracing these unique attributes that you bring to the table. It's about understanding that being a perfectionist is not a flaw, but rather a strength. Your attention to detail, organization, drive for excellence, high standards, detail-oriented nature, and strong work ethic are all qualities that should be celebrated.

Next time someone criticizes your perfectionist tendencies, remember these unique attributes and be proud of who you are. Your commitment to excellence is what sets you apart from others, and it should be embraced and celebrated. So go ahead and continue striving for perfection; it's what makes you, you.

Finding Peace And Joy By Leveraging The Power Of Perfectionism In A Healthy Way

You take pride in your work and accomplishments, but at the same time, you struggle with the constant pressure to be perfect. It's a never-ending cycle of chasing perfection and feeling like you're never quite good enough.

But what if I told you that being a perfectionist doesn't have to be a burden? In fact, embracing your inner drive for excellence can bring a sense of peace and joy to your life. It's all about finding a healthy balance and using the power of perfectionism to your advantage, such as;

Embrace Your Perfectionism, It's A Powerful Attribute

First and foremost, stop seeing your perfectionism as a flaw. Instead, recognize it as a valuable attribute that can help you reach your full potential. Perfectionists are known for being detail-oriented, organized, and committed to achieving their goals. These are all qualities that can lead to success in both personal and professional aspects of life.

It's important to realize that perfectionism isn't the same as perfection. Perfection is an unattainable goal, whereas perfectionism is a healthy drive for excellence. Embrace your perfectionism and use it as a motivation to constantly improve and do your best.

Set Realistic Goals:
One of the downsides of being a perfectionist is setting unrealistic expectations for yourself. You may have a vision of perfection in your mind, but you have to understand that it's not always possible to achieve that level of perfection. Instead, set realistic goals that push you to do better while also being attainable.

Start by making a list of your goals and break them down into smaller, more manageable tasks. This will help you to see progress and feel a sense of accomplishment along the way. And don't be too hard on yourself if you don't reach your goal right away. Perfection is a process, and every step you take towards it is a success.

Learn to Let Go

One of the biggest challenges for perfectionists is letting go of things that are not perfect. It can be difficult to accept that things may not always go as planned or turn out exactly as we imagined. However, it's important to understand that imperfection is a part of life and can even lead to new and unexpected opportunities.

Practice accepting imperfection and learning to let go of things that are outside of your control. This will not only help you find peace with your perfectionism but also save you from unnecessary stress and anxiety.

Celebrate Your Accomplishments:

Perfectionists tend to be extremely hard on themselves, always focusing on what they could have done better. It's important to take a step back and recognize your achievements. Acknowledge the hard work and effort you put into something, and celebrate your successes, no matter how big or small they may be.

This will help you to appreciate your strengths and abilities, and it's also a great way to boost your self-esteem. Remember, it's okay to be proud of yourself and give yourself credit where credit is due.

Practice Self-Care:
Lastly, as a perfectionist, it's crucial to prioritize self-care. It's easy to get caught up in the pursuit of perfection and forget about your own well-being. Make time for activities that bring you joy and relaxation. This could be anything from spending time in nature, reading a book, or practicing mindfulness and meditation. Taking care of your mental, emotional, and physical health is vital for finding balance and happiness in your life.

By embracing your inner drive for excellence

and finding a healthy balance, you can use your perfectionism to your advantage. Remember to prioritize self-care and enjoy the journey to perfection, rather than solely striving for the end result. With these tips, you can find peace and joy in your perfectionism and live a fulfilling life.

Becoming Your Own Biggest Ally By Understanding And Embracing Your Perfectionist Tendencies

You stand in front of the mirror, analyzing every inch of your appearance. Tucking and adjusting every strand of hair until it's in the perfect place. As you head out for work, you triple-check your to-do list, making sure everything is in order. You strive for perfection in everything you do, and nothing short of it will suffice. If this sounds like you, then congratulations, you're a perfectionist.

But being a perfectionist isn't always easy. While

striving for excellence can bring great success, it also comes with its own set of challenges. The constant pressure to be perfect can lead to burnout, anxiety, and an overwhelming fear of failure. However, instead of viewing these tendencies as a hindrance, why not embrace them and use them to your advantage? By understanding and accepting your perfectionist tendencies, you can become your own biggest ally and reach your full potential.

First and foremost, it's important to acknowledge that being a perfectionist is not a flaw. It simply means you have high standards for yourself and strive for excellence. It's a trait that sets you apart from others and can be a powerful tool if used correctly. By accepting this part of yourself, you can let go of any negative associations and start viewing it in a positive light.

Next, it's crucial to understand that perfection is subjective. What may seem like perfection to you may not be the same for someone else. Acknowledge that there will always be room for improvement, and that's okay. Instead of striving for a flawless outcome, learn to accept and appreciate your efforts and progress along the way.

The key to embracing your perfectionist tendencies is learning to manage them effectively. Set realistic goals that push you out of your comfort zone, but are still attainable. Be mindful of your self-talk and make sure it's encouraging and supportive rather than self-critical. When you feel yourself getting overwhelmed, take a step back and give yourself a break. Remember, perfectionism is about progress, not perfection.

It's also essential to recognize that failure is a natural part of the journey to success. Embracing your perfectionist tendencies means understanding that failure is not the end result, but merely a stepping stone towards improvement. Thomas Edison famously said, 'I have not failed. I've just found 10,000 ways that won't work.' Adopting this mindset can help you view failures as opportunities for growth and learning.

Finally, surround yourself with a support system that understands and accepts your perfectionist qualities. Seek out mentors or friends who can provide guidance and encouragement along your journey. Sharing your struggles and successes with like-minded individuals can help you feel less alone and more supported.

Understand that perfection is subjective, manage your tendencies effectively, embrace failure as a part of growth, and surround yourself with a supportive community. By doing so, you can become your own biggest ally and reach your full potential. So go out there and let your inner perfectionist shine!

CHAPTER 6

TOOLS FOR TRANSFORMATION

As a perfectionist, you are no stranger to the constant striving for excellence. It is a part of your inner drive, a fundamental belief that fuels your actions and pushes you forward. But as you continue on this pursuit of perfection, you may find yourself encountering obstacles and challenges that seem insurmountable or hard to overcome.

The first tool for transformation is self-awareness. As a perfectionist, you are acutely aware of your strengths and weaknesses, and this can be a double-edged sword. On one hand, it allows you to set realistic goals and strive for improvement. On the other hand, it can lead to self-criticism and a fear of failure. To address this, take time to reflect on your thought patterns and how they affect your behavior. Do you tend to focus on your mistakes or your achievements? By becoming more aware of these patterns, you can start to challenge them and reframe your thoughts in a more positive light.

Next, embrace imperfection. This may sound contradictory to your perfectionist nature, but accepting that you are not perfect and that mistakes are a natural part of growth is crucial for your well-being. Instead of striving for perfection, aim for progress and growth. Understand that making mistakes and facing challenges are opportunities for learning and development. This mindset shift can help alleviate the constant pressure you put on yourself and allow you to enjoy the journey towards excellence.

Another valuable tool for transformation is setting realistic goals. Perfectionists tend to set impossibly high standards, which can be demotivating when they are not met. Instead, break down your goals into smaller, achievable steps. This will not only make them more manageable, but also give you a sense of accomplishment and motivation to keep going. Remember, perfection is not a destination, it is a continuous journey.

Practice self-compassion. As a perfectionist, you may be your own worst critic, constantly berating yourself for not meeting your high standards. This can be emotionally draining and detrimental to your self-esteem. Instead, treat yourself with kindness and understanding, just as you would a friend. Acknowledge that it is okay to make mistakes and be patient with yourself as you work towards your goals.

Finally, embrace a growth mindset. Researcher Carol Dweck coined the terms 'fixed mindset' and 'growth mindset' to describe two different mindsets when it comes to success and failure. A fixed mindset believes that our abilities and intelligence are fixed traits and cannot be developed, while a growth mindset believes that they can be developed through hard work and dedication. Embracing a growth mindset allows us to see challenges as opportunities for growth and encourages us to keep trying despite setbacks.

Being a perfectionist is not a flaw, but it can be a hindrance if not managed properly. By incorporating these tools for transformation into your life, you can embrace your inner drive for excellence in a healthy and fulfilling way. Remember, perfection is not the ultimate goal, but rather continuous growth and progress. So go out there and use these tools to transform your perfectionism into a positive force in your life.

Practical strategies for working with perfectionism.

You've always been a perfectionist. From a young age, you strived for excellence in everything you did. Your school assignments had to be flawless, your room had to be spotless, and your artwork had to be perfect. While others may have praised you for your high standards, you knew deep down that your perfectionism wasn't always a positive trait. It caused you stress and anxiety, and you often found yourself stuck in a cycle of self-criticism and self-doubt.

But what if your perfectionism could be harnessed in a positive way? What if you could use it as a tool to achieve excellence without letting it control your life? The good news is, it is possible. Below are ways to embrace your inner drive for excellence and find balance in your perfectionism.

1. Set realistic expectations

As a perfectionist, you have likely set impossibly high expectations for yourself. While these standards may motivate you to work hard, they can also lead to feeling overwhelmed and burnt out. Take a step back and assess whether your goals are realistic and achievable. This doesn't mean lowering your standards, but rather setting attainable and meaningful goals.

2. Celebrate small wins

Perfectionists tend to focus on what they haven't accomplished rather than celebrating what they have achieved. Make a conscious effort to recognize and appreciate your small wins. It could be completing a task ahead of schedule or receiving positive feedback from a colleague. Celebrating these victories will help boost your confidence and keep you motivated.

3. Practice self-compassion

Perfectionists often have a harsh inner critic that constantly judges their every move. It's important to develop a more compassionate and understanding inner voice. Treat yourself with the same kindness and forgiveness that you would offer a friend. Remember, perfection is an unattainable goal, and it's okay to make mistakes.

4. Break tasks into smaller steps

Perfectionists tend to take on too much at once, leading to overwhelm and procrastination. Break down your tasks into smaller, more manageable steps. This will make the process less intimidating and help you stay on track. As you complete each step, you'll feel a sense of accomplishment and keep your momentum going.

5. Embrace imperfection

Perfectionists have a hard time accepting anything less than perfect. But the truth is, imperfection is a natural part of the human experience. Embrace it and see it as an opportunity to learn and grow. Giving yourself permission to make mistakes will help release the pressure you put on yourself.

6. Focus on progress, not perfection

Instead of fixating on the end result, focus on the progress you're making. Set realistic and measurable goals and track your progress along the way. This will help you see how far you've come and motivate you to keep going.

7. Practice mindfulness

Perfectionism often stems from a fear of failure

or not being good enough. Practicing mindfulness can help you become aware of these thoughts and challenge them. It can also help you stay present and appreciate the journey without getting caught up in perfectionism.

8. Seek support

Perfectionism can be hard to overcome on your own. Consider seeking support from a therapist or joining a support group for perfectionists. Talking to others who understand your struggles can provide validation and motivation to make positive changes.

Remember, perfectionism is a part of who you are, but it doesn't have to control your life. Use these practical strategies to harness your inner drive for excellence and find balance in your perfectionism. Embrace your imperfections and see them as opportunities for growth and learning. You'll be amazed at the positive impact it will have on your life.

Identifying personal perfectionist archetypes.

If you are reading this, chances are you are a perfectionist or know someone who is. Being a perfectionist can be both a blessing and a curse. On one hand, it motivates you to be the best version of yourself and strive for excellence in everything you do. On the other hand, it can also lead to a constant feeling of never being satisfied and always striving for an unattainable level of perfection.

But have you ever stopped to think about what type of perfectionist you are? Yes, you heard that right. There are different types, or archetypes, of perfectionists. Each one has their own set of strengths and weaknesses, and understanding which type you are can help you make the most of your perfectionist traits.

The first step in identifying your personal perfectionist archetype is to understand the common traits and behaviors associated with each one.

1. The Standard Setter

You have high standards for yourself and constantly strive to meet or exceed them. You have a strong work ethic and are often perceived as reliable and responsible. However, you can also be overly critical of yourself and others when these standards are not met.

2. The Procrastinator

You have a fear of failure and perfectionism often paralyzes you from taking action. You might spend excessive amounts of time preparing and planning but struggle to actually start or complete tasks. This can lead to missed opportunities and feelings of guilt and shame.

3. The Overachiever

You have a need for external validation and constantly push yourself to achieve more. You are driven and ambitious, but can also become burnt out and overwhelmed by the pressure to constantly succeed.

4. The Fixer

You have a strong desire to improve and fix things, whether it's your personal life or the world around you. While this can lead to great accomplishments, the constant need for improvement can also create feelings of dissatisfaction and never feeling good enough.

5. The People Pleaser

You have a strong desire to please others and avoid conflict at all costs. This can lead to taking on too much and sacrificing your own needs and priorities. You may struggle with setting boundaries and saying no, leading to burnout and resentful feelings.

6. The Status Seeker:

Do you strive for perfection to impress others or gain external validation? You might be the High Achiever, driven by a need for recognition and accomplishment.

7. The Worrier's :

Does your perfectionism stem from a fear of failure and its consequences? You could be the Anxious Perfectionist, constantly seeking to avoid mistakes.

8.The Controller:

Do you find comfort in order and predictability? You might be the Architect, meticulously planning and executing to maintain a sense of control.

9. The Idealist:

Do you have a strong internal compass for what's "right"? You could be the Crusader, driven by a personal vision of flawlessness and a desire to create a perfect world.

10. The Self-Critic:

You have an internal voice that constantly berates you for not meeting impossibly high standards. You are hyper-aware of your flaws and mistakes, viewing them as evidence of your inadequacy or unworthiness. This inner critic can be relentless and debilitating, leading to feelings of shame, guilt, and self-doubt.

11. The All-or-Nothing Thinker:

You see the world in black and white terms, believing that if something isn't perfect, it's a total failure. This leads to unrealistic expectations and a tendency to give up easily when things don't go as planned.

Now that you have a general understanding of the different perfectionist archetypes, it's time to determine which one resonates with you the most. Think about your thoughts, behaviors, and feelings in different situations. Which archetype do you identify with the most? It's important to note that you may identify with more than one archetype, and that's completely normal.

Once you have identified your personal

perfectionist archetype, it's important to embrace it and use it to your advantage. Each archetype has its own strengths, and by harnessing them, you can achieve great things. However, it's also important to be aware of the potential pitfalls and negative patterns associated with your type.

For example, if you are a Standard Setter, focus on setting realistic and achievable goals rather than perfection. If you are a Procrastinator, try breaking tasks into smaller, manageable steps and remind yourself that mistakes are a part of the learning process. The key is to find a healthy balance between striving for excellence and letting go of the need for perfection.

Remember, embracing your perfectionism is not about changing who you are, but rather learning to work with it and use it to your advantage. By understanding your personal perfectionist archetype, you can take control of your inner drive for excellence and achieve your goals while still prioritizing your well-being and mental health.

Learning to navigate stress and anxiety with self-compassion.

The constant pressure to be perfect can lead to self-doubt, self-criticism, and relentless worrying. You may have been told to just "relax" or "don't be so hard on yourself," but it's not that simple for someone like you. So how do you navigate stress and anxiety with self-compassion?

First, it's important to acknowledge that perfectionism is not an inherently bad trait. In fact, it can be a great motivator and drive for success. The problem arises when it becomes all-consuming and detrimental to our well-being. So the first step is to accept and embrace your inner drive for excellence, but also recognize when it's becoming too much.

Next, it's important to understand that you are not alone. Many perfectionists struggle with stress and anxiety, and it's nothing to be ashamed of. It's essential to have a support system of friends, family, or a therapist who can help you navigate these challenges and provide a safe space to express your fears and concerns without judgment.

Learning to practice self-compassion is also crucial in managing stress and anxiety. As a perfectionist, you tend to hold yourself to impossibly high standards and criticize yourself harshly when you don't meet them. But self-compassion teaches us to be kind and understanding to ourselves, just as we would to a friend who is going through a tough time. So the next time you feel overwhelmed, try talking to yourself as you would to a friend - with understanding, kindness, and encouragement.

Another helpful tool in managing stress and anxiety is to reframe your thinking. As a perfectionist, you may have a tendency to catastrophize and think of the worst-case scenario when faced with a challenge. But instead, try to focus on the present moment and view obstacles as opportunities to learn and grow. Remember that it's not about being perfect, but about being resilient and finding the courage to keep going.

Lastly, don't forget to take care of yourself. While your drive for excellence may push you to keep going and ignore your own needs, it's important to prioritize self-care. This can mean setting boundaries, taking breaks, and engaging in activities that bring you joy and relaxation.

Learning to navigate stress and anxiety with self-compassion is the key to maintaining balance and well-being. Remember to accept and embrace your inner drive for excellence, seek support when needed, practice self-compassion, reframe your thinking, and prioritize self-care. With these tools, you can embrace your perfectionism while also managing stress and anxiety in a healthy way. You've got this, perfectionist. Keep striving for excellence, but don't forget to be kind to yourself along the way.

Embracing imperfection as a part of the human experience.

Picture this; you're walking through a bustling city street, surrounded by a sea of faces, each one with their own unique story to tell. As you navigate through the crowds, you can't help but notice the imperfections that make each person beautiful in their own way – the crooked smiles, the laugh lines etched around their eyes, the scars that tell tales of battles won and lost.

In this moment, you realize that imperfection is not something to be feared or avoided – it's a fundamental part of what it means to be human. It's what makes us unique, what gives us character and depth. It's the messy, chaotic, wonderfully imperfect journey of life that makes it worth living.

Embracing imperfection is about letting go of the need to be flawless and instead embracing the beauty of being perfectly imperfect. It's about accepting yourself – flaws and all – and recognizing that your worth is not determined by your ability to meet impossible standards of perfection.

Think about the most memorable moments in your life – the ones that have touched your heart and soul in a profound way. Chances are, they were not moments of perfection, but rather moments of raw authenticity and vulnerability. They were moments when you allowed yourself to be seen, flaws and all, and were met with love, acceptance, and understanding.

Embracing imperfection is about letting go of the pressure to be perfect and instead embracing the messy, beautiful journey of self-discovery and growth. It's about recognizing that life is not about reaching some unattainable standard of perfection, but rather about embracing the journey – with all its ups and downs, twists and turns.

So the next time you find yourself striving for perfection, take a moment to pause and reflect on the beauty of imperfection. Embrace your flaws, your quirks, your scars – they are what make you uniquely you. And remember, it's not about being perfect – it's about being perfectly imperfect, and finding beauty in the messiness of life.

CHAPTER 7

OVERCOMING CHALLENGES

You have always been known as a perfectionist. From a young age, you strived for excellence in everything you did. You were never satisfied with anything less than perfection and you pushed yourself to your limits to achieve it. While your drive for excellence may have led to great success and accolades, it has also brought its fair share of challenges.

As you embark on your journey to embrace your inner drive for excellence, you will inevitably face challenges along the way. These challenges may seem hard, but with the right mindset and strategies, you can overcome them and continue on your path towards perfection.

One of the biggest challenges you will face as a perfectionist is the fear of failure. The thought of not meeting your own high standards is enough to send you into a spiral of anxiety and self-doubt. You may have a constant fear of disappointing yourself and others, leading you to shy away from taking risks and trying new things. However, it is important to remember that failure is a natural part of any journey towards excellence. Embracing failure as a learning opportunity rather than a reflection of your worth will allow you to push past your fear and continue striving for perfection.

Another challenge that perfectionists often face is the never-ending pursuit of perfection. You may find yourself constantly setting higher and higher standards for yourself, never truly feeling satisfied with your achievements. This constant chase for perfection can lead to burnout and feelings of inadequacy. Learning to recognize and appreciate your achievements, even if they are not perfect, is crucial in overcoming this challenge. Celebrate your progress and acknowledge that perfection is not always attainable.

Perfectionists also tend to be extremely self-critical. You may be your own harshest critic, constantly finding flaws and mistakes in your work. This constant inner dialogue of self-criticism can be draining and demotivating. To overcome this challenge, it is important to practice self-compassion. Treat yourself with the same kindness and understanding that you would offer to a friend or loved one. Remember that mistakes are a natural part of growth and that being kind to yourself will only make you stronger.

In addition to internal challenges, you may also face external challenges as a perfectionist. Others may not understand your drive for excellence and may question your methods or criticize your efforts. This can be discouraging and may make you doubt yourself. However, it is important to stay true to yourself and your goals. Surround yourself with supportive and understanding individuals who will encourage and inspire you on your journey.

As a perfectionist, you may also struggle with prioritizing and time management. With your high standards, you may find yourself wanting to perfect every little detail, leading to an overwhelming workload. Learning to prioritize and manage your time effectively is key in overcoming this challenge. Identify your most important tasks and focus on them first, rather than getting lost in minor details. Set realistic goals and deadlines for yourself, and don't be afraid to delegate tasks if needed.

Lastly, it is important to recognize that perfectionism, if left unexamined, can turn into an unhealthy obsession. It can lead to feelings of constant stress and anxiety, and can even negatively impact your mental health. It is crucial to find a balance between striving for excellence and taking care of your well-being. Make time for activities and relationships that bring you joy and help you relax. Remember that perfection is not the ultimate goal, and that happiness and fulfillment are just as important.

Overcoming the challenges of perfectionism may not be easy, but with determination and self-awareness, it is possible. Embrace your inner drive for perfection and success , but also learn to let go and be kind to yourself. By overcoming these challenges, you will not only become a better perfectionist, but also a happier and healthier individual. So keep pushing forward, and may your journey towards perfection be a fulfilling one.

Exploring the challenges associated with perfectionism.

You are a highly driven individual with a strong desire for success and achievement. You have always prided yourself on your perfectionistic tendencies, always striving for excellence in everything you do. However, in recent times, you have begun to notice that this perfectionism comes with its own set of challenges. You have found yourself constantly pushing yourself beyond your limits, never feeling satisfied with your accomplishments, and feeling intense pressure to meet impossibly high standards.

Perfectionism can be defined as a tendency to set extremely high standards for oneself and to strive for flawlessness in everything. On the surface, this may seem like a positive trait to possess. After all, who wouldn't want to be perfect? However, the reality is far more complex and can be detrimental to one's mental and emotional well-being.

One of the main challenges of perfectionism is the constant feeling of never being good enough. You set impossibly high standards for yourself and when you inevitably fall short, you feel like a failure. This can lead to a cycle of self-doubt and self-criticism, causing you to question your worth and abilities. It can also lead to extreme perfectionistic procrastination, where the fear of not meeting your own expectations paralyzes you from taking action.

Another challenge is the constant need for

control. As a perfectionist, you want everything to be perfect and you believe that you are the only one who can make it happen. This can lead to difficulty in delegating tasks to others and micromanaging every aspect of your life. This need for control can also extend to relationships, causing strain and pushing loved ones away. Constantly striving for perfection in all areas of life can also lead to burnout and physical health problems.

Furthermore, perfectionism can also lead to problems with decision-making. The fear of making a mistake or making the wrong choice can paralyze you and prevent you from taking action. You may spend excessive amounts of time analyzing and overthinking every decision, leading to a lack of progress and missed opportunities. This can also lead to a fear of failure and a reluctance to take risks, hindering personal and professional growth.

Perfectionism can also have a detrimental effect on your mental health. The constant pressure to be perfect can lead to anxiety, depression, and other mental health issues. It can also cause a negative self-image, as you constantly compare yourself to an unattainable standard. This can lead to feelings of inadequacy and low self-esteem, which can impact all areas of your life.

So, how can you navigate these challenges associated with perfectionism? The first step is to recognize that perfectionism is not a healthy or sustainable mindset. Acknowledge that striving for excellence is a positive trait, but aiming for perfection is not. Realizing that perfection is an impossible standard to achieve can help you shift your perspective and set more realistic expectations for yourself.

You can also challenge your perfectionistic thoughts and behaviors by setting more flexible and achievable goals. Instead of aiming for perfection, aim for progress. This can help you break the cycle of self-criticism and allow yourself to celebrate your accomplishments, no matter how small.

Another important aspect is self-compassion. Be kind to yourself and practice self-care. Treat yourself with the same level of care and understanding that you would extend to a loved one. Accept that mistakes are a natural part of the learning process and give yourself permission to make them.

Surrounding yourself with supportive and understanding people can also be helpful in managing perfectionism. Seek out individuals who appreciate your strengths but also understand and accept your flaws. These relationships can provide a sense of validation and help you see yourself in a more realistic and positive light.

Lastly, seeking professional help can also be beneficial if you find yourself struggling to manage your perfectionism. A therapist or coach can help you identify and challenge the root causes of your perfectionistic tendencies, and provide you with tools and strategies to cope with them.

Strategies for overcoming setbacks and setbacks.

You have always been a perfectionist. From a young age, you strived for perfection in everything you did. You aimed for straight A's in school, put in extra hours at work, and meticulously planned every aspect of your life. Your drive for excellence and perfection has brought you much success, but it has also come with its fair share of setbacks.

Setbacks are a natural part of life. They are the unexpected obstacles that challenge our plans and force us to adjust our course. For the perfectionist, setbacks can be particularly challenging. They can cause feelings of failure, disappointment, and even self-doubt. However, with the right strategies, you can learn to overcome setbacks and use them as an opportunity for growth and improvement.

Types of Setbacks

It is important to first understand the types of setbacks that a perfectionist may encounter. These setbacks can be categorized into two main types – internal and external setbacks.

Internal setbacks are those that are caused by your own thoughts and feelings. As a perfectionist, you have high expectations for yourself, and when things don't go according to plan, you may be overly critical of yourself. This can lead to self-doubt, anxiety, and a fear of failure.

External setbacks, on the other hand, are caused by circumstances outside of your control. These can include things like unexpected events, changes in plans, or other people's actions. For a perfectionist, external setbacks can be frustrating and disheartening as they disrupt the carefully planned and executed steps to achieve a goal.

Both internal and external setbacks can be challenging to overcome, but with the right strategies, you can learn to navigate them successfully.

Strategies for Overcoming Setbacks

1. Acknowledge Your Feelings

The first step in overcoming setbacks is to acknowledge and accept your feelings. As a perfectionist, you may have a tendency to suppress your emotions or push them aside in order to keep pushing forward. However, this can be counterproductive as your feelings will likely resurface later. Take some time to identify and process your emotions. Whether it is disappointment, frustration, or self-doubt, allow yourself to feel these emotions without judgment.

2. Reframe Your Perspective

When facing a setback, it is common to focus on

the negative aspects of the situation. However, this only serves to increase our feelings of disappointment and frustration. Instead, try to reframe your perspective and find the positive aspects of the setback. What have you learned? How can this setback help you grow and improve? Reframing your perspective can help you see setbacks as opportunities for growth and development rather than failures.

3. Seek Support

It can be helpful to talk to someone about your setbacks. This could be a friend, family member, or even a therapist. Talking about your feelings with someone who understands and supports you can help you process your emotions and gain a different perspective on the situation. They can also offer encouragement and help you come up with a plan to move forward.

4. Practice Self-Compassion

Perfectionists can be their own harshest critics.

When facing a setback, it is important to practice self-compassion. Treat yourself with the same kindness and understanding that you would offer to a friend in a similar situation. Remind yourself that setbacks are a natural part of life and that you are doing the best you can.

5. Focus on What You Can Control

Although setbacks may be out of our control, we can still choose how we respond to them. Focus on the things that you can control – your attitude, your actions, and your mindset. Replace negative thoughts with positive ones and take action towards your goals in a way that feels manageable and realistic.

6. Learn From Your Setbacks

Setbacks can be valuable learning experiences. Take some time to reflect on what went wrong and what you can do differently in the future. This will not only help you avoid similar setbacks in the future but also help you grow and improve as a perfectionist.

7. Take Breaks and Practice Self-Care

Constantly striving for perfection can be mentally and emotionally draining. It is important to take breaks and practice self-care to recharge and refocus. This could be engaging in activities that bring you joy, practicing mindfulness or relaxation techniques, or simply taking time for yourself. This will help you maintain balance and prevent burnout.

8. Keep Pushing Forward

It can be tempting to give up and abandon your goals when faced with setbacks, but remember that setbacks are just temporary roadblocks. As a perfectionist, your drive for excellence will continue to push you forward. Use these setbacks as motivation to keep pushing towards your goals and remember that setbacks can ultimately lead to greater success and improvement.

Therefore, setbacks are a natural part of life and learning to overcome them is essential for any perfectionist.With these strategies, you can become an even more resilient and successful perfectionist.

Cultivating resilience in the face of adversity.

You have always prided yourself on your high standards and your relentless pursuit of excellence.

But as you grew older, you realized that life isn't always smooth sailing. Adversities and challenges are inevitable, and they can throw a wrench in your pursuit of perfection. These obstacles can range from minor setbacks to major crises, and they can leave you feeling defeated and unmotivated. However, as a perfectionist, you know that giving up is not an option. You are determined to overcome any roadblocks and continue striving for excellence.

So, buckle up and get ready to strengthen your resilience to overcome any challenges that come your way, so let's start with Understanding Resilience.

Before we discuss the ways to cultivate resilience, it's important to understand what resilience is. Simply put, resilience is the ability to bounce back from adversity. It is the capacity to recover and adapt in the face of challenges, hardships, and trauma. Resilience is not something you are born with; it is a skill that can be developed and honed over time.

As a perfectionist, you may already possess some degree of resilience. After all, your determination and persistence in achieving your goals can be seen as a form of resilience. However, to truly cultivate resilience, you need to dig deeper and develop a more holistic approach towards approaching challenges, Such as :

1. Acknowledge Your Emotions

The first step towards building resilience is acknowledging and accepting your emotions. As a perfectionist, you may have a tendency to suppress your emotions and put on a brave front, even in the face of adversity. While this may seem like the right thing to do, it can actually hinder your resilience in the long run.

Allow yourself to feel and express your emotions, whether it's anger, frustration, sadness, or fear. These emotions are a natural response to difficult situations, and suppressing them can lead to more stress and emotional exhaustion. Instead, validate and accept your feelings, and then work towards finding healthy ways to cope with them.

2. Practice Self-Compassion

Self-compassion is often overlooked, but it is a crucial element in cultivating resilience. As a perfectionist, you may be harsh and critical towards yourself, especially when things don't go according to plan. However, this negative self-talk can be damaging to your resilience.

Instead, practice self-compassion by treating yourself with kindness and understanding. Acknowledge that you are human and that making mistakes is a part of the learning process. Treat yourself with the same kindness and compassion you would show to a loved one in a similar situation.

3. Set Realistic Goals

As a perfectionist, you are probably used to setting high goals for yourself. While ambitious goals can be motivating, they can also backfire when faced with adversity. When your goals are unrealistic, it can lead to disappointment and frustration, making it difficult to bounce back.

It's important to set goals that are challenging, yet achievable. By setting realistic goals, you can also celebrate small victories along the way, which can boost your confidence and motivation.

4. Have a Strong Support System

Having a strong support system is crucial for cultivating resilience. Surrounding yourself with people who believe in you and offer their support can help you navigate through adversity. Whether it's friends, family, or a mentor, having someone to lean on and share your struggles with can make a world of difference.

Additionally, it's essential to surround yourself with people who inspire and motivate you. Whether it's through their achievements or their resilience in the face of adversity, being around positive influences can help you cultivate your own resilience.

5. Embrace Change and Adaptability

As a perfectionist, you may be set in your ways and resistant to change. However, in the face of adversity, change is inevitable. Being adaptable and open to change can help you navigate through difficult situations and come out stronger on the other side.

Be open to different perspectives and be willing to try new approaches if your initial plan doesn't work out. Remember, change is not a sign of weakness; it's a sign of growth and resilience.

6. Seek Professional Help

Despite your best efforts, sometimes adversity can be overwhelming, and you may need additional support. Seeking professional help is a sign of strength, not weakness. A therapist or a counselor can provide you with the tools and strategies to cope with adversity and build your resilience.

With that being said , being a perfectionist can bring immense satisfaction and success, but it also comes with its own set of challenges, especially when faced with adversity. However,

resilience is not about eliminating all struggles –
it's about bouncing back stronger and wiser.

CHAPTER 8

NAVIGATING RELATIONSHIPS

Are you someone who constantly strives for perfection in every aspect of your life? Do you set high standards for yourself and those around you? If so, then you are a perfectionist. While many view perfectionism as a positive quality, it can also come with its own set of challenges, especially when it comes to navigating relationships.

It's no secret that perfectionists can have a difficult time maintaining healthy and satisfying relationships, whether it be with friends, family, or romantic partners. Your constant need for control and perfection can take a toll on those around you, leading to conflict and resentment. But don't worry, it's not all doom and gloom. By understanding the root causes of your perfectionism and learning how to manage it within your relationships, you can create stronger and more fulfilling connections.

First and foremost, it's important to acknowledge that your drive for excellence and perfectionism stem from a deep-rooted fear of failure and rejection. You constantly feel the need to prove yourself and your worth through your achievements and the approval of others. While this may bring temporary satisfaction, it can also create a never-ending cycle of stress and pressure. It's crucial to address these insecurities and learn how to prioritize your own well-being over external validation.

One of the key aspects of navigating relationships as a perfectionist is to understand that perfection is not attainable, especially in relationships. People are not perfect, and therefore, relationships cannot be either. Instead of striving for perfection, aim for growth and improvement. By accepting that mistakes and imperfections are a natural part of any relationship, you can learn to let go of unrealistic expectations and appreciate the journey.

Communication is also a crucial factor in any relationship, especially for perfectionists. Your desire for control can often lead to difficulties in expressing your thoughts and emotions. You may fear vulnerability and rejection, and therefore, avoid conflict and difficult conversations. However, this can lead to pent-up resentments and misunderstandings. It's important to practice open and honest communication, even when it feels uncomfortable. Remember, healthy relationships are built on trust and understanding.

Additionally, as a perfectionist, you may have a tendency to be hyper-critical of yourself and others. While your intentions may be rooted in a desire for excellence, constantly nitpicking and criticizing can be damaging to relationships. Instead, try to focus on giving constructive feedback and acknowledging the efforts of both yourself and others. Learn to embrace and appreciate imperfections, as they can often lead to growth and learning.

Another important aspect of navigating relationships as a perfectionist is learning to manage your expectations. It's natural to have expectations in any relationship, but when they are too rigid and unattainable, they can lead to disappointment and frustration. Learn to set realistic expectations and be flexible when things don't go exactly as planned. This will help you avoid unnecessary stress and conflict in your relationships.

Lastly, remember to prioritize self-care and self-compassion in your relationships. As a perfectionist, you may have a tendency to put others' needs above your own, leading to burnout and resentment. It's important to set boundaries and take time for yourself to recharge. Learn to be kind to yourself and practice self-forgiveness when things don't go perfectly. This will not only benefit your mental well-being but also strengthen your relationships in the long run.

We all know that being a perfectionist can be both a blessing and a curse in relationships. While it's important to aim for perfection , it's equally important to recognize and manage the challenges it can bring in your relationships. So go forth, dear perfectionist, and master the art of relationships. Your inner drive for perfection will only make them even more special.

Understanding the impact of perfectionism on personal relationships.

A perfectionist can be identified from the way they dress to the way they approach their work. They have high standards for themselves and strive for excellence especially in everything they do.

Perfectionism is often seen as a positive trait, a desire for flawless performance and achievement. However, it can also be a double-edged sword, leading to feelings of inadequacy, anxiety, and loneliness. As a perfectionist, you may constantly feel the need to control every aspect of your life, including your relationships. This can put a strain on your friendships, romantic relationships, and even your relationship with yourself.

One of the key impacts of perfectionism on personal relationships is the constant need for approval and validation. Because you set such high standards for yourself, you may expect the same level of perfection from others. This can lead to feelings of disappointment and frustration when they do not meet your expectations. You may also have a difficult time accepting criticism or constructive feedback, as it may be seen as a personal failure.

Your perfectionism may also make it challenging for you to be vulnerable in relationships. You may fear revealing your flaws and weaknesses, as it goes against your pursuit of perfection. This can create a distance between you and your loved ones, as they may feel like they are unable to fully connect with you.

In addition, your perfectionist tendencies may lead to a lack of empathy and understanding towards others. You may be highly critical of those who do not meet your standards, leading to conflicts and strained relationships. Your focus on perfection can also make it difficult for you to see things from others' perspectives, which is crucial in any healthy relationship.

When it comes to romantic relationships, perfectionism can be especially damaging. Your high expectations may put a lot of pressure on your partner, making them feel like they are always walking on eggshells around you. Your need for control and lack of vulnerability may also make it challenging for them to feel emotionally connected to you. Over time, this can create resentment and a sense of disconnection in the relationship.

Moreover, your pursuit of perfection can also lead to an unhealthy push for your partner to change and meet your high standards. This can be damaging for both you and your partner, as it can create feelings of inadequacy and insecurity. It is important to remember that nobody is perfect, and expecting your partner to be flawless will only lead to disappointment and strain in the relationship.

Finally, your perfectionism may also impact your relationship with yourself. As you strive for perfection, you may become self-critical and judgmental of your own abilities and actions. This can lead to feelings of low self-esteem and self-doubt, which can impact your overall well-being. It is important to acknowledge that perfection is unattainable and to learn to embrace your imperfections.

Understanding the impact of perfectionism on personal relationships is the first step towards building healthier, more fulfilling connections with others. While being a perfectionist may bring success and achievements in your career, it is important to recognize the impact it can have on your personal relationships.

Strategies for fostering healthy connections while managing perfectionist tendencies.

Sometimes, your inner drive for perfection can become overwhelming, affecting your relationships and overall well-being. Does it sound familiar to you? If so, then this strategy is for you .

Being a perfectionist can bring many benefits – dedication, attention to detail, and a strong work ethic, to name a few. However, it can also bring about feelings of stress, self-doubt, and constant pressure to meet impossible standards. It is important to find a balance between striving for excellence and maintaining healthy connections with others. Here, we will explore some strategies for managing perfectionist tendencies while fostering healthy relationships.

1. Recognize your perfectionist tendencies

The first step in managing your perfectionist tendencies is to recognize and acknowledge them. Often, perfectionism can be deeply ingrained in our personalities and we may not even realize the extent of it. Take some time to reflect on your behavior and thought patterns. Do you often feel disappointed when you don't meet your own expectations? Do you have a hard time delegating tasks because you believe you are the only one who can do them perfectly? These are just some examples of perfectionist tendencies. By becoming more aware of them, you can start to challenge them and make changes.

2. Set realistic goals

Perfectionists tend to set high, often unachievable standards for themselves. While it's great to have ambitious goals, it's important to make sure they are realistic and attainable. Break down large goals into smaller, more manageable ones. This will not only help you stay on track, but also give you a sense of accomplishment when you reach each milestone. Remember, perfection is not attainable, and striving for it can lead to burnout and disappointment.

3. Embrace imperfection

As hard as it may be, try to embrace imperfection. Remember that perfection is subjective and what may be perfect for you may not be for someone else. Instead of fixating on flaws, focus on progress and growth. Accept that mistakes will be made and use them as opportunities to learn and improve. Trying to be perfect all the time is exhausting and can prevent you from enjoying the present moment.

4. Practice self-compassion

Perfectionists tend to be harsh critics of themselves. Instead of beating yourself up for not meeting your own expectations, practice self-compassion. Treat yourself with the same kindness and understanding you would a friend or loved one. Give yourself credit for your efforts and achievements and don't be too hard on yourself when things don't go as planned.

5. Communicate openly

Perfectionists often have a hard time expressing their thoughts and feelings, especially when it comes to admitting mistakes or asking for help. However, healthy relationships require open and honest communication. If you are feeling overwhelmed or struggling with perfectionism, don't be afraid to reach out to a trusted friend or family member. Talk to them about your feelings and work together to find a solution.

6. Set Boundaries

Boundaries are important for everyone, but especially for perfectionists. Set realistic expectations for yourself and others and learn to say no when you feel overwhelmed. It's also important to set boundaries with others when it comes to their expectations of you. Let them know that while you strive for excellence, perfection is not your priority and you need their support and understanding.

7. Seek professional help

If your perfectionism is causing significant distress in your life and relationships, seeking professional help may be beneficial. A therapist can help you identify underlying factors contributing to your perfectionist tendencies and teach you healthy coping mechanisms. They can also provide a safe space for you to explore and challenge your thoughts and beliefs.

Being a perfectionist is not necessarily a bad thing. However, when it starts to affect your relationships and well-being, it's important to take steps to manage it. Remember to be kind to yourself, embrace imperfection, and communicate openly with others. With these strategies, you can foster healthy connections and find a balance between your drive for excellence and living a fulfilling life.

Communication techniques for expressing needs and boundaries.

If you are a perfectionist, driven by a strong desire to achieve perfection in everything you do, even in your work, relationships, and personal life. Then, you know that being a perfectionist can have its challenges, especially when it comes to communication and expressing your needs and boundaries.

As a perfectionist, you often have high expectations for yourself and those around you. You may find it difficult to express your needs and boundaries because you fear being seen as demanding or difficult. This can lead to feelings of frustration and resentment, as your needs go unmet and your boundaries are crossed. The key is learning how to communicate effectively and assertively, without sacrificing your perfectionist tendencies.

The first step in effective communication is to recognize and acknowledge your needs and boundaries. Take some time to reflect on what is important to you, what you need in your relationships, and what your limits are. This will allow you to more clearly communicate your needs and boundaries to others.

Next, learn to express yourself assertively. As a perfectionist, you may struggle with being direct and asserting yourself. You may fear conflict or worry about hurting others' feelings. However, assertiveness is a crucial skill in communication, and it does not have to be aggressive or confrontational. It simply means expressing yourself in a clear and respectful manner.

When communicating your needs and boundaries, use 'I' statements to take ownership of your feelings and avoid blaming others. For example, instead of saying 'You never listen to me,' you could say, 'I feel like my opinions are not being heard.' This approach avoids putting the other person on the defensive and allows for a more productive conversation.

Another important technique is active listening. As a perfectionist, you may have a tendency to focus on getting your point across rather than truly listening to others. Active listening involves giving your full attention, maintaining eye contact, and acknowledging what the other person is saying. This shows that you value their perspective and encourages open communication.

It is also crucial to set boundaries and stick to them. This may be challenging for a perfectionist, but it is essential for maintaining healthy relationships. Be clear and specific about what you are comfortable with and what you are not. Setting and enforcing boundaries may feel uncomfortable at first, but it is necessary for your well-being.

Finally, learn to be forgiving and flexible. As a perfectionist, you may have a hard time accepting imperfection, whether in yourself or others. However, it is important to recognize that everyone makes mistakes and that not everything will go exactly as planned. Practice being forgiving and flexible, and use mistakes as learning opportunities rather than reasons for disappointment.

Also, being a perfectionist does not mean sacrificing your communication skills. Remember, effective communication is a two-way street, so be open to listening and understanding others' needs and boundaries as well. With practice, you can maintain your high standards while also maintaining healthy relationships and boundaries.

CHAPTER 9

EMBRACING SELF-COMPASSION

You are an achiever. Everything you do, from your work to your hobbies, is done with impeccable attention to detail and a drive for perfection . This perfectionist mindset has brought you success and recognition, but it has also come at a cost – your self-compassion.

Constantly striving for perfection can be exhausting and overwhelming. When you make a mistake or fall short of your own expectations, you are quick to criticize yourself and beat yourself up. You view any form of failure as a personal flaw, rather than a natural part of the learning process. This lack of self-compassion can lead to feelings of worthlessness and burnout, despite your achievements.

But what if I told you that you can still be a

perfectionist and embrace self-compassion at the same time? It may seem counterintuitive, but practicing self-compassion can actually enhance your drive for excellence and help you maintain a healthier and more balanced perspective on your achievements.

So, how do you embrace self-compassion as a perfectionist? The first step is to understand what self-compassion really means. It is the act of treating yourself with the same kindness, care, and understanding that you would offer to a loved one in a similar situation. It involves acknowledging your own humanity and accepting that mistakes and imperfections are a normal part of life.

To illustrate this, let's imagine that you have spent hours working on a project, but it does not turn out as perfectly as you wanted. As a perfectionist, your initial reaction may be to berate yourself and criticize your efforts. But with self-compassion, you would pause and acknowledge that it's okay to make mistakes and that your worth as a person is not defined by this one project. You would offer yourself kind words of encouragement and remind yourself that mistakes are opportunities for growth and learning.

Another important aspect of self-compassion is to give yourself permission to take breaks and prioritize self-care. As a perfectionist, you may feel guilty or lazy for taking breaks when there is still work to be done. But the truth is, breaks are essential for maintaining your mental and physical well-being. It allows you to recharge and come back to your work with renewed focus and energy. Remember, you are not a machine – you deserve rest and self-care, just like anyone else.

Embracing self-compassion also means letting go of the need for external validation. As a perfectionist, you may constantly seek approval and recognition from others. But true self-worth comes from within, not from the praise of others. Instead of relying solely on external validation, remind yourself of your own values and motivations. Set your own personal goals and celebrate your progress and growth, rather than waiting for the approval of others.

Lastly, it's important to practice self-compassion in moments of failure or setbacks. As a perfectionist, you may see failure as a personal reflection of your abilities and feel like giving up. But with self-compassion, you can view failure as a valuable lesson and an opportunity to improve. It's about being understanding and forgiving towards yourself, rather than being self-critical and harsh.

Therefore, embracing self-compassion as a perfectionist means finding a balance between striving for excellence and being kind to yourself. It's about acknowledging your own humanity and accepting that you are not perfect. It's about prioritizing self-care and setting your own personal standards, rather than relying on external validation. And most importantly, it's about being kind and understanding towards yourself in moments of failure and setbacks. So go ahead, embrace your desire for perfection , but remember to also embrace your need for self-compassion.

Cultivating self-compassion as a counterbalance to perfectionism.

The word 'perfectionist' often brings to mind images of impeccably organized desks, pristine white walls, and a never-ending pursuit of flawlessness. While striving for excellence and attention to detail can be admirable qualities, the dark side of perfectionism can lead to feelings of self-doubt, anxiety, and ultimately, burnout. As a perfectionist, you understand the constant pressure to excel in all aspects of your life, from your career to your relationships. But what if there was a way to balance your drive for perfection with self-compassion? This is where cultivating self-compassion becomes a powerful tool for the perfectionist.

As a perfectionist, you hold yourself to

impossibly high standards and often beat yourself up when you inevitably fall short. You may constantly compare yourself to others and feel inadequate when you perceive them as achieving more or being more successful. This unrelenting pursuit of perfection can lead to a constant feeling of never being good enough, no matter how much you achieve or how hard you work.

Cultivating self-compassion involves shifting your perspective from one of self-judgment to one of self-kindness. Instead of criticizing yourself for your mistakes or perceived shortcomings, you learn to treat yourself with the same kindness and understanding that you would show a close friend or family member. Self-compassion involves acknowledging your imperfections and mistakes, but not letting them define your self-worth.

One of the key components of self-compassion is practicing self-acceptance. This means accepting yourself as you are, flaws and all. As a perfectionist, this can be a difficult concept to grasp, as you may constantly strive for self-improvement. However, accepting yourself as you are does not mean you are complacent or unwilling to change. It simply means that you acknowledge that you are a human being, with strengths and weaknesses, and that you are deserving of love and compassion, just like everyone else.

Self-compassion also involves being mindful of your thoughts and emotions. As a perfectionist, you may have a tendency to overthink or catastrophize situations, leading to heightened levels of stress and anxiety. By practicing mindfulness, you can learn to observe your thoughts and emotions without judgment, and then let them go. This can help you to avoid getting caught up in a vicious cycle of self-criticism and doubt.

In addition to mindfulness, self-compassion also involves being kind to yourself. This can involve simple acts of self-care, such as taking a break when you are feeling overwhelmed, treating yourself to something you enjoy, or speaking to yourself in a kind and supportive manner. As a perfectionist, you may have a critical inner voice that constantly points out your flaws and shortcomings. By actively practicing self-kindness, you can begin to quiet this inner voice and replace it with more positive and encouraging self-talk.

Another important aspect of self-compassion is recognizing that you are not alone in your struggles. As a perfectionist, you may feel like you are the only one who experiences feelings of self-doubt and anxiety. However, the truth is that many people struggle with similar feelings. By acknowledging this, you can cultivate a sense of common humanity, which can help to alleviate feelings of isolation and self-judgment.

By embracing self-compassion, you can counterbalance the negative effects of perfectionism. When you practice self-compassion, you are more likely to experience greater emotional well-being, reduce feelings of anxiety and depression, and increase your resilience in the face of setbacks. So the next time your perfectionistic tendencies start to take over, remember to embrace your inner need for perfection , but also extend kindness and understanding to yourself. You deserve it.

Practicing mindfulness and self-care to promote mental well-being.

Are you tired of constantly pushing yourself to be perfect? Do you feel overwhelmed by the pressure to always achieve excellence in every aspect of your life? It's time to take a step back and embrace your need for perfection in a healthier way.

First and foremost, it is important to understand that perfection is unattainable. No matter how hard we try, there will always be room for improvement or someone who is better. Instead of striving for perfection, focus on growth and progress. Set realistic goals and celebrate your achievements, no matter how small they may seem.

One of the key elements of practicing mindfulness is being present in the moment. As a perfectionist, it's easy to get caught up in future goals and past mistakes, causing unnecessary stress and anxiety. By focusing on the present, you can let go of any expectations and appreciate your current journey. Take a few moments each day to meditate, journal, or simply sit quietly and clear your mind. This will help you become more self-aware and in tune with your inner thoughts and feelings.

In addition to being present, it's important to practice self-compassion. Perfectionists tend to be their own worst critics and can be extremely hard on themselves. Instead of beating yourself up for any perceived failures, practice self-compassion by treating yourself with kindness and understanding. Treat yourself the way you would treat a friend who is going through a difficult time. Remember, making mistakes is a part of the learning and growth process.

Another aspect of self-care is taking care of your physical well-being. A healthy body leads to a healthy mind. Make time for regular exercise and proper nutrition. Don't view it as a chore, but instead, find an activity that you enjoy and look forward to. It could be something as simple as taking a daily walk or joining a dance class. Also, make sure to prioritize your sleep. As a perfectionist, you may have a tendency to overwork and sacrifice sleep to meet your goals. However, a good night's rest is crucial for your mental and physical health.

It's also important to set boundaries for yourself. As a perfectionist, you may have a hard time saying no and taking on too much. Learn to recognize when you are feeling overwhelmed and learn to say no to things that are not a priority in your life. Create a balance between work and leisure activities. Taking breaks and doing activities that bring you joy will help prevent burnout and promote a healthier mindset.

Lastly, seek support from others. As a perfectionist, you may feel like you have to do everything on your own. However, it's important to recognize that everyone needs support and it's okay to ask for help. Surround yourself with a supportive network of friends and family who understand you and your perfectionist tendencies. Seek therapy or support groups if needed. Remember, it takes strength to acknowledge and ask for help when you need it.

Embracing your need for perfection does not have to come at the cost of your mental well-being. By practicing mindfulness and self-care, you can achieve a healthier balance and lead a more fulfilling life. You deserve to live a life filled with joy and self-acceptance.

Recognizing the inherent worthiness of oneself, regardless of achievements.

You have always been a perfectionist. From a young age, you have always wanted to be the best in school, in sports, in your career. You pushed yourself to the limits, always seeking to achieve more, to be better than anyone else. However, as you grew older, you began to realize that this pursuit of perfection was taking a toll on you. You felt anxious, stressed, and constantly judged yourself harshly for not meeting your own impossibly high standards.

It's time to take a step back and reassess your mindset. As a perfectionist, you are driven by the need to achieve, to be perfect in everything you do. But at what cost? It can be easy to get caught up in the pursuit of perfection and forget about the importance of self-worth and self-acceptance. It's time to let go of the idea that your worth is based on your achievements. It's time to embrace your inner drive for excellence while recognizing the inherent worthiness of yourself, regardless of your accomplishments.

It's important to understand that self-worth is not attached to external factors such as success, wealth, or status. You are worthy, simply because you exist. Your value as a person does not diminish if you make a mistake or fail to reach a goal. Your worth is not based on what others think of you, but rather, how you think of yourself.

Take a moment to reflect on your accomplishments. Perhaps you have achieved great success in your career or have received recognition for your talents and skills. While it's important to be proud of these achievements, it's equally important to recognize that they do not define you as a person. You are more than your job, your accomplishments, or your talents. You are a talented individual with unique qualities, flaws, and experiences that make you who you are.

Embracing your inner drive for perfection does

not mean letting go of your high standards or ambition. It means understanding that perfection is not attainable and that it's okay to make mistakes. It's about learning to appreciate the journey towards a goal, rather than just the end result. It's about being kinder to yourself, forgiving yourself for your imperfections, and understanding that failure is a part of growth and progress.

Recognizing your inherent worthiness also means valuing yourself beyond your achievements. Take the time to focus on self-care and self-love. This could be through daily positive affirmations, setting aside time for hobbies and activities that bring you joy, or spending quality time with loved ones. When you prioritize your well-being and happiness, you will find that your drive for excellence comes from a place of self-fulfillment rather than the need to prove yourself to others.

As you continue on your journey as a perfectionist, remember that it's okay to strive for excellence, but also important to recognize your worth beyond your achievements. You are capable, talented, and deserving of love, respect, and success, regardless of your level of perfection. Embrace your inner drive for excellence and perfection , but also embrace yourself for who you are – perfectly imperfect.

CHAPTER 10

EMBRACING IMPERFECT ACTION

You stand at the starting line, ready to begin another project. Your mind is buzzing with ideas and your heart is filled with determination. You have high expectations for yourself, and you know that you will push yourself to achieve nothing less than perfection.

As a perfectionist, you are driven by an insatiable desire for excellence. You strive to reach the highest levels of success in every aspect of your life. You set lofty goals for yourself and work tirelessly to achieve them. While this drive for perfection can lead to incredible accomplishments, it can also come with its own set of challenges.

One of the biggest challenges for a perfectionist

is the fear of failure. You are so focused on achieving perfection that the thought of making a mistake or falling short of your expectations is terrifying. This fear can often lead to procrastination, as you wait until the perfect moment to begin, or it can lead to paralysis where you are unable to take any action at all.

However, there is a powerful mindset shift that can help you overcome this fear and allow you to embrace your intended desire for perfection : the concept of embracing imperfect action.

Embracing imperfect action means acknowledging that not everything you do will be perfect and that is okay. It means allowing yourself to take action, even if you are unsure if it will lead to success. It is about embracing the process of learning and growing, rather than solely focusing on the end result.

By embracing imperfect action, you free yourself from the paralyzing fear of failure. You give yourself the permission to make mistakes and learn from them. You understand that failure is not a reflection of your worth or abilities, but an opportunity to grow and improve.

Embracing imperfect action also allows you to break free from the shackles of perfectionism. As a perfectionist, you may find yourself getting caught up in small details, trying to make everything flawless. This can lead to spending an excessive amount of time on one task, to the detriment of other responsibilities and goals. Embracing imperfect action helps you let go of that need for perfection and allows you to focus on achieving your goals in a more efficient and effective manner.

Moreover, embracing imperfect action fosters creativity and innovation. When you are not constrained by the need for perfection, you are open to exploring new ideas and trying new approaches. This can lead to breakthroughs and unexpected successes that you may have missed if you were solely focused on achieving perfection.

To truly embrace imperfect action, you must also learn to let go of the need for external validation. As a perfectionist, you may constantly seek approval and praise from others. However, by accepting that not everything you do will be perfect, you also accept that not everyone will approve of or appreciate your efforts. This allows you to focus on your own personal growth and satisfaction, rather than seeking validation from external sources.

Embracing imperfect action takes courage and a willingness to let go of the need for perfection. It may not come easily, but with practice and persistence, it can become a powerful tool in your arsenal as a perfectionist. So, the next time you find yourself hesitating to take action for fear of failure or imperfection, remember to embrace imperfect action and see where it takes you. You may just be surprised at the results.

Embracing the concept of "good enough" instead of striving for perfection.

You have always been someone who strives for perfection, you always want to drive for perfection that is unmatched. You have spent countless hours pouring over details and perfecting every aspect of your life.

While your drive for perfection has led to many successes, it has also come with a cost. You are always stressed, anxious, and constantly striving for more. You put immense pressure on yourself to be flawless and this can often lead to feelings of disappointment and frustration when things don't go according to plan.

But what if I told you that there is an alternative to this never-ending pursuit of perfection? What if you could embrace a new concept and find peace and satisfaction in simply being 'good enough'?

It may sound counterintuitive, but embracing the idea of 'good enough' can actually lead to greater happiness and fulfillment in life. Instead of constantly chasing the unattainable, you can learn to appreciate and celebrate your efforts and achievements.

Firstly, it's important to understand that perfection is a subjective concept. What may seem perfect to one person, may not be to another. This means that your pursuit of perfection is essentially chasing an ever-changing and elusive goal. By accepting that perfection is not a realistic or even desirable goal, you can free yourself from the never-ending cycle of striving and disappointment.

Embracing 'good enough' also means accepting that mistakes and imperfections are a natural part of life. They are opportunities to learn and grow, rather than signs of failure. By allowing yourself to make mistakes and not expecting perfection, you can find a sense of freedom and relief from the constant pressure to be flawless.

Moreover, constantly striving for perfection can also lead to an unhealthy and unbalanced lifestyle. It's important to recognize that some things simply don't require perfection. For example, spending excessive amounts of time and energy on a project at work may mean sacrificing time with loved ones or self-care activities. Embracing the concept of 'good enough' allows you to prioritize and find a healthy balance in all aspects of your life.

It's also crucial to understand that perfectionism can often stem from a fear of failure or a need for external validation. By embracing 'good enough' and learning to trust in your own abilities and efforts, you can find a greater sense of self-confidence and self-worth. Your value does not depend on being perfect, and by accepting this, you can find a newfound sense of inner peace and self-acceptance.

Of course, this doesn't mean that you should stop striving for perfection altogether. It simply means finding a healthy perspective and balance. Striving for perfection is a positive trait, but it should not come at the expense of your mental and emotional well-being.

In addition , embracing the concept of 'good enough' allows you to let go of the constant pursuit of perfection and find a greater sense of contentment and fulfillment in life. It may take time to shift your mindset, but by learning to appreciate your efforts and achievements, rather than fixating on flaws and mistakes, you can find a more balanced and happier way of living. So, the next time you feel the pressure to be perfect, remember that sometimes, good enough is more than good enough.

Encouragement to take imperfect action and embrace the learning process.

Imagine standing at the edge of a very big ocean, the waves crashing against the shore with relentless determination. Each wave represents a new opportunity, a chance to dive into the unknown and embrace the journey of learning and growth. As you look at the horizon, you feel a mixture of excitement and apprehension, unsure of what lies beneath the surface. But deep down, you know that this is where true growth and transformation lie – in taking imperfect action and embracing the learning process.

You've spent so much of your life striving for perfection, seeking to achieve flawless results in everything you do. But perfection is a mirage, a shimmering illusion that recedes further into the distance with each step you take towards it. In your quest for perfection, you've overlooked the beauty of imperfection – the messy, chaotic, wonderfully imperfect journey of learning and growth.

It's time to let go of your fear of imperfection and embrace the learning process with open arms. Instead of waiting for the perfect moment or the perfect opportunity, take imperfect action and trust that you will learn and grow along the way. Allow yourself to make mistakes, to stumble and fall, knowing that each misstep brings you one step closer to your goals.

Embracing the learning process is about shifting your mindset from one of fear and perfectionism to one of curiosity and resilience. It's about recognizing that failure is not a reflection of your worth, but rather a natural part of the journey towards success. Every setback, every obstacle, is an opportunity to learn, to adapt, and to grow stronger.

So take that first step into the unknown, knowing that you may stumble along the way. Embrace the uncertainty, the discomfort, the messiness of the learning process. Trust in your ability to navigate the waves of change and emerge stronger and more resilient on the other side.

And remember, you are not alone on this journey. Surround yourself with a supportive community of friends, mentors, and fellow travelers who can offer guidance, encouragement, and perspective along the way. Lean on them for support when you need it, and offer support in return. Together, you can weather any storm and emerge stronger and more resilient than ever before.

So dive into the ocean of learning with courage and conviction. Take imperfect action, embrace the journey, and trust in your ability to navigate the waves of change. And remember, it's not about reaching the perfect destination – it's about enjoying the journey and embracing the beauty of imperfection along the way.

Celebrating progress over perfection and finding joy in the journey.

Picture walking along a winding forest path, the sunlight filtering through the canopy above, dappling the ground with patches of golden light. Each step you take brings you closer to your destination, but it's not the destination that matters – it's the journey itself, the winding path of twists and turns, ups and downs, that fills you with a sense of wonder and awe.

For so long, you've been chasing after perfection, striving to achieve flawless results in everything you do. But perfection is like a distant star, always just out of reach, no matter how fast you run or how hard you try. In your pursuit of perfection, you've overlooked the beauty of progress – the small victories, the incremental steps forward, that add up to something truly remarkable.

It's time to shift your focus from perfection to progress, from the destination to the journey itself. Instead of fixating on the end goal, celebrate the progress you've made along the way. Every step forward, no matter how small, is a cause for celebration – a testament to your strength, resilience, and determination.

Finding joy in the journey is about embracing the present moment, savoring the sights, sounds, and sensations that surround you. It's about finding beauty in the mundane, the ordinary, the everyday moments that make life worth living. Whether it's the feel of the sun on your face, the sound of birdsong in the trees, or the taste of fresh air in your lungs, there is joy to be found in every moment, if only you take the time to notice.

So celebrate your progress, no matter how small. Take a moment to reflect on how far you've come, the obstacles you've overcome, and the growth you've experienced along the way. Whether it's mastering a new skill, reaching a milestone, or simply showing up and putting in the work each day, every step forward is a victory to be celebrated.

And remember, the journey is not meant to be perfect. There will be bumps in the road, detours, and setbacks along the way. But these challenges are not obstacles to be feared or avoided – they are opportunities for growth, learning, and self-discovery. Embrace them with an open heart and a curious mind, knowing that each challenge you face makes you stronger and more resilient in the end.

So let go of your attachment to perfection and embrace the beauty of progress. Celebrate each step forward, no matter how small, and find joy in the journey itself. For it is in the journey that true happiness lies, not in the destination

CONCLUSION

As you stand at the crossroads of your journey towards self-acceptance, you can't help but marvel at how far you've come. What once seemed like an insurmountable obstacle – the relentless pursuit of perfection – has transformed into a powerful ally on your path to growth and fulfillment.

Reflecting on your transformation, you can't help but smile at the journey you've been on. You've shifted from viewing perfectionism as a flaw to embracing it as a superpower; a force that drives you to strive for excellence, but also empowers you to embrace imperfection and find beauty in the messy, chaotic journey of life.

Along the way, you've learned to embrace the different types of perfectionist personalities, recognizing that each one brings its own strengths and challenges. From the messy perfectionist to the procrastinator to the Parisian perfectionist, you've discovered that there is no

specific approach to perfectionism. Instead, you've learned to steer perfectionism in a positive way, harnessing its energy and drive to propel you forward on your journey.

But perhaps most importantly, you've embraced self-acceptance; the realization that you are worthy and deserving of love and belonging exactly as you are. You've learned to celebrate the journey towards a balanced and joyful life, knowing that perfectionism is not a flaw to be fixed, but a guiding force that can lead you towards your fullest potential.

As you look ahead to the road still stretching out before you, you do so with a sense of excitement and anticipation. You know that there will be challenges and obstacles along the way, but you also know that you have the resilience, the strength, and the support to overcome them. And so you step forward, ready to embrace the journey with open arms, knowing that perfectionism will be by your side every step of the way, guiding you towards a life filled with balance, joy, and self-acceptance.